To my daughters, Allison and Melissa,

May you seek knowledge and pursue compassion,

May the love and joy you have given me surround you all your days,

And may your faith rise above any challenges.

QUESTIONING

Your

DOUBTS

A Harvard PhD Explores Challenges to Faith

CHRISTINA M. H. POWELL

IVP Books

An imprint of InterVarsity Press
Downers Grove, Illinois

InterVarsity Press
P.O. Box 1400, Downers Grove, IL 60515-1426
www.ivpress.com
email@ivpress.com

InterVarsity Press® is the book-publishing division of InterVarsity Christian Fellowship/USA®, a movement of students and faculty active on campus at hundreds of universities, colleges and schools of nursing in the United States of America, and a member movement of the International Fellowship of Evangelical Students. For information about local and regional activities, visit www.intervarsity.org.

All Scripture quotations, unless otherwise indicated, are taken from THE HOLY BIBLE, NEW INTERNATIONAL VERSION®, NIV® Copyright © 1973, 1978, 1984, 2011 by Biblica, Inc.™ Used by permission. All rights reserved worldwide.

Published in association with the literary agency of WordServe Literary Group, Ltd., 10152 Knoll Circle, Highlands Ranch, CO 80130.

While all stories in this book are true, some names and identifying information in this book have been changed to protect the privacy of the individuals involved.

Cover design: Cindy Kiple
Interior design: Beth McGill
Images: Joel Carillet/Getty Images

ISBN 978-0-8308-3678-9 (print)
ISBN 978-0-8308-9671-4 (digital)

Printed in the United States of America ∞

Library of Congress Cataloging-in-Publication Data
Powell, Christina M. H., 1967-
Questioning your doubts : a Harvard PhD explores challenges to faith
/ Christina M. H. Powell.
pages cm
Includes bibliographical references.
ISBN 978-0-8308-3678-9 (pbk. : alk. paper)
1. Faith. I. Title.
BV4637.P675 2014
234'.23—dc23

2014024727

P	21	20	19	18	17	16	15	14	13	12	11	10	9	8	7	6	5	4	3	2	1
Y	32	31	30	29	28	27	26	25	24	23	22	21	20	19	18	17	16	15	14

Contents

INTRODUCTION

ONE HUNDRED BILLION NEURONS wired for action are poised on top of your shoulders. Each of these neurons makes an average of 7,000 connections with other neurons in your brain. With a total number of connections ranging from 100 trillion to 500 trillion,[1] you wake up each morning ready to let the creative sparks fly!

Considering that the lowly nematode, a transparent roundworm about one millimeter long, possesses only 302 neurons,[2] human beings can rejoice in their generous endowment of thinking capacity. With our ability to think comes our propensity to ask questions. Our questions move beyond the simple, where's lunch? of most creatures. As human beings, we think with enough sophistication to speculate on the purpose for our existence and the future direction of the universe. We are self-aware even if we often remain unaware of our human limitations. Not content to simply forge tools and plant crops, we create art, ponder philosophy and develop theology.

CENTRAL TO OUR IDENTITY

Our thinking is central to our identity as human beings. Our mental capacities, such as consciousness, memory, reasoning and imagination, distinguish us from all other animals. As the noted neuroscientist Pasko T. Rakic once stated, "The brain is the organ that sets us apart from any other species. It is not the strength of our muscles or of our bones that makes us different, it is our brain."[3]

Researchers sometimes uncover certain aspects of human thinking in other animals. For example, self-awareness, as measured by the ability to recognize oneself in a mirror, may be present in orcas, bottlenose dolphins, elephants, European magpies and great apes as well as in human beings. Some animals, such as rats, fish, birds and monkeys, have the capacity, as humans do, to navigate using landmarks and the shape of the environment. For many years scientists believed that only humans possessed episodic memory, a category of long-term memory that involves recollection of specific events you have personally experienced, such as passing your driving test, your high school graduation or the birth of your first child. Yet experiments within the past ten years suggest that scrub jays, chimpanzees and gorillas may be able to recall past events and use the information to make better choices in the future. Animals such as chimpanzees, rhesus macaques and tamarins may possess nonlinguistic mathematical ability, defined as the ability to compare numbers and perform simple addition in the absence of language skills.

While other animals may possess some of the mental capabilities of humans, including self-awareness, the sum total of human mental capabilities remains unique. The Christian who acknowledges God as the Creator must conclude that humans truly were created to think. The believer must then contemplate what role this God-given thinking ability should play in a person's journey of faith.

CRUCIAL QUESTIONS

Our thinking ability leads us to ask questions, including crucial ones about faith. In a world where science has succeeded in offering explanations for most phenomena in the universe, we may wonder if belief is plausible. In the midst of natural disasters, suffering and injustice, we may wonder if God truly cares about us. How can we know if God is real?

The answers to these crucial questions require a balance between faith and reason, feeling and thinking. To be intellectually responsible, Christians must be willing to face the difficult questions about their faith. However, intellectual responsibility also requires a commitment to question doubts in all the various forms in which they may arise.

TAXONOMY OF DOUBTS

Doubts come in many varieties, and the approach to dealing with doubts varies according to the category of a given doubt. Some doubts are intellectual, asking age-old questions such as, How can we believe in the goodness of God while thousands are killed in tsunamis and earthquakes? If God is all-powerful, why does he allow evil to flourish in this world? Why does God create people he knows will reject him? These intellectual doubts can move from the abstract to the personal, becoming experiential doubts, such as, Why didn't God protect my brother from dying in the car accident? Why did God allow my friend to become a rape victim? Why doesn't God bring someone into the life of my son to help him return to church?

These intellectual and experiential doubts can be faith crippling if left unaddressed. Other less serious doubts involve the normal life adjustment of expectations and experiences. Did I choose the right major? Should I switch jobs? Is this person the one I should marry? Sometimes these doubts are beneficial, helping a person choose the right direction in life. Doubts that lead to discernment serve as warning flags of caution, alerting a person to the need to look closer at a problem or a situation in order to avoid making a mistake that would lead to greater difficulties with the passage of time.

Some doubts help you solve problems while others are only a symptom of a lack of confidence. Doubts that produce problem-solving insights often are doubts based on knowledge and probability, reflecting a measure of the degree of uncertainty you have regarding empirical evidence or the soundness of a logical argument. Self-doubts that diminish a person's confidence have an emotional component. Research on metacognition, the process of thinking about one's own mental processes, shows that doubting your doubts can lead to more confidence.[4] Interestingly, sports psychology research shows that a little self-doubt can improve athletic performance.[5] While second-guessing yourself or others too much can be immobilizing, a dose of humility plus a dash of self-awareness can be a recipe for success.

FAITH AS A PROCESS

Whether you are experiencing a potentially faith-crippling doubt about the existence or goodness of God, a doubt about your life direction, or a doubt about your own ability to accomplish a certain task, this book will help you think through your doubts, understand the various sources of doubts and work toward resolving those doubts.

In the first part of this book, we will explore the idea that God created us to think, and try to find the right balance between relying on our intellect and recognizing its limits. We will also examine the interplay of influences that shape our beliefs in order to become better equipped to question doubts arising from our background, our cognitive biases, and the positive and negative influences of people in our lives. Some doubts, like the ones that help us discover a problem before it becomes serious, can be beneficial. We will consider how questions can help us solve problems and differentiate between doubts that help us correct our course in life and doubts that tear down our faith and our confidence. We will learn how to ask questions to gather information, deepen our relationships, defeat false assumptions and achieve greater focus when pursuing goals.

In the second part of the book, we will explore several sources of doubts. In chapter five, we will consider how some doubts spring from limitations in our human abilities, lifespan and academic disciplines, such as science and theology. Sometimes a person needs to summon the courage to push past limits in life while at other times a person needs to exercise patience and wait for new opportunities. We will consider examples of both situations and discuss ways to discern which approach is appropriate to a given set of circumstances. In chapter six, we will take a look at doubts that arise from unanswered questions in life. We will take into account the place for mystery in our understanding of the universe and our response to art. We will tackle the problem of human suffering and find practical ways to help people experiencing grief after a tragedy. We will see how God's timing connects the experience of closed doors to the promise of fulfilled dreams.

In chapter seven, we will discuss doubts born from pain. If a person has a wrong view of God, painful circumstances can trigger a crisis of faith. However, suffering also can deepen a person's faith and serve as preparation for ministry to others. The difference in outcome results from the approach a person takes to processing grief and the accompanying doubts. In chapter eight, we will explore doubts that are disillusionment in disguise. To varying degrees, we all harbor comforting illusions about our churches, workplaces, educational institutions and relationships that challenging life experiences can shatter. We can become frustrated and disillusioned when we discover the imperfections that mar the ideals we hold. In processing the doubts we experience after a disillusioning experience, we can become like a pendulum swinging from one extreme to the other. When our disillusioning experience involves the church or our concept of God, we can reject our faith in the aftermath. However, the end result of disillusionment need not be cynicism. We can choose to become a catalyst for the change we would like to see in our churches and communities, setting realistic yet significant goals toward a better tomorrow.

In the third part of the book, we will look at different approaches to implement in resolving doubts. In chapter nine, we will explore how authentic faith pervades everyday life, lives in the moment and develops over time. In chapter ten, we will examine the value of recalling our journey of faith to gain resources to handle our present and future questions, doubts and challenges. In chapter eleven, we will consider the approach of handling doubts in the context of community, learning from believers around us as well as the Christian community throughout the ages and throughout the world. In chapter twelve, we will see how our journey of faith is an incomplete process, sending us through the cycle of questioning, examining and resolving doubts many times during our life. Finally, we will explore how our efforts at gaining and maintaining spiritual health can have a larger effect on the community around us.

My goal in writing this book is to provide you with tools you can use to understand and resolve the doubts that arise in the course of living life as a Christian. While you will find answers in this book, my desire is to impart to you more than mere information, for I know that tomorrow will bring new questions, necessitating the process of seeking new answers. I have chosen to teach you how to fish, instead of cooking you a fish dinner. Question your faith if you must, but do not neglect the responsibility of questioning your doubts!

Part One

THINKING THROUGH DOUBTS

1

CREATED TO THINK

But what, then, am I?

A thinking thing, it has been said.

But what is a thinking thing?

It is a thing that doubts, understands,

conceives, affirms, denies, wills, refuses;

that imagines also, and perceives.

RENÉ DESCARTES, "MEDITATION II"

Jesus replied, "Love the Lord your God with all your heart
and with all your soul and with all your mind."

MATTHEW 22:37

"A FIRE ON THE HEARTH SIGNIFIES HOME, and here is a home
for Harvard men. I hope this fire will burn bright every winter
evening, and that it will burn long for comfort and for light." On
November 12, 1913, Harvard president A. Lawrence Lowell spoke
these words and lit the first fire in the great fireplace of the new Main
Clubhouse of the Harvard Club of Boston.

"Straight ahead," said a man dressed in crisp black trousers and a crimson jacket with black cuffs. "You will find the coat-check room to the right of Harvard Hall Foyer." Following his directions, I entered the foyer then stopped to take in my new surroundings. Gentlemen from the beginning of the twentieth century cast glances from their places on the dark-paneled walls. Crimson carpeting extended from the Harvard Hall ballroom to the grand staircase leading to the Massachusetts and Aesculapian rooms upstairs. Soothing strains of classical music played by a pianist and a harpist wafted from Harvard Hall. I felt the richness of history and the weight of expectations combine with the cocoonlike comfort of home. I stood in an exclusive sanctuary secluded from the bustle of the city of Boston just outside the heavy wooden doors.

I hesitated for a moment before sitting in a Queen Anne chair near the fireplace. At the age of twenty-five, I had become a member of the Harvard Club of Boston, a place that only started to admit women the year I entered kindergarten. The quiet grandeur of the Harvard Club of Boston made me question whether I belonged there, while beckoning me to make myself at home. I sank into the chair. I closed my eyes, rested my head on the wing of the chair and stretched my legs toward the warmth of the fireplace. The soft glissandos from the harp washed away the pressures of Harvard Medical School.

Adjusting to life as a graduate student at Harvard went beyond developing a taste for Earl Grey tea, fine dining and ornate architecture. As a professing Christian conducting scientific research, I found myself inhabiting two different worlds. Take a trip to the end of the aisles in the science section of any local bookstore, and you will find several new releases promoting the popular notion of irresolvable conflict between theology and science. Listen to sermons emanating from many evangelical pulpits, and you may come to believe that too much education can destroy a person's faith.

Isaac Newton, one of the most influential scientists who ever lived, was also a Christian theologian. He once said, "We build too many walls and not enough bridges." Curious how I remained a Christian while studying science, friends and acquaintances would ask me, "Have you ever questioned your faith?" In an attempt to build a bridge between the world of faith and reason, I would answer, "Sure, I question my faith, but I also question my doubts."

Faith is described as "confidence in what we hope for and assurance about what we do not see" (Heb 11:1). Faith goes beyond the limits of human reasoning. Doubts, however, are the results of human reasoning. The seventeenth-century French philosopher and father of analytical geometry René Descartes would describe doubts as the products of "thinking things." In other words, your ability to think creates your capacity to doubt. When I stood next to the chair by the Harvard Club fireplace and questioned whether I belonged in my new environment, I was experiencing doubt. This doubt was the appropriate target for questioning, not the faith that had brought me thus far.

Of course, scientists and academics are not the only ones that people assume must question their faith. I have heard people ask Christians going through difficult life circumstances this same question. Maybe people assume faith is nothing more than an assurance of personal happiness or a guarantee of success that hardships and heartaches can expose as false. Possibly faith is a mere illusion that tough times can strip away. Sometimes we need to build a bridge over the gap between our expectations and our experiences.

CONSTRUCTING NEWTON'S BRIDGE

Isaac Newton's assertion that we should build more bridges than walls resonates with me because bridges filled the landscape of my childhood. I spent the first eighteen years of my life growing up in the City of Bridges. Pittsburgh, Pennsylvania, contains within its city limits more bridges than Venice, Italy, with the current number of bridges totaling nearly two thousand. Three major rivers come together at the Point, the location of Pittsburgh's iconic fountain, first built in 1974. These rivers, along with the steep hills and ravines around the city, make bridges a necessity for transportation. The early European settlers of Pittsburgh quickly learned that they had to choose between living in isolation and finding creative ways to span the waters and valleys.

People cluster on one of two riverbanks in their approach to relating human reasoning to faith. The first approach, common in many Christian circles in my childhood and college years and persisting to this day, revolves around mistrust of the intellect. Acquiring knowledge, analyzing information and questioning assumptions become suspect activities. Too much thinking means you are not listening to your heart, you are out of touch with practical concerns or you are not truly spiritual.

Many Christians find support for mistrusting the intellect in a variety of biblical passages. Beginning in Eden, Eve's temptation included a desire for wisdom and knowledge. Proverbs 3:5, an often-quoted verse, says,

Trust in the LORD with all your heart
    and lean not on your own understanding.

In the New Testament we read that Jesus said to the doubting apostle Thomas, "Because you have seen me, you have believed; blessed are those who have not seen and yet have believed" (John 20:29). In a letter to the Corinthians, the apostle Paul explained, "But God chose the foolish things of the world to shame the wise; God chose the weak things of the world to shame the strong" (1 Cor 1:27).

We find clustered on the second riverbank those who worship the life of the mind above all else. Human reasoning reigns supreme. The standard for judging truth becomes data collected through the human senses and processed by rational thought. Atheists and agnostics wield Ockham's razor to slice away the possibility of revelation, preferring explanations that avoid spirituality. While the fourteenth-century Franciscan friar William of Ockham was right to suggest that a scientific model should avoid introducing more causes than necessary, the principle often is used to exclude from the possibility of existence everything not perceivable by the human senses. Ockham's razor is a sound approach to the practice of science, but when brandished too freely, justifies positivism. This philosophy persuades those who dwell on the second riverbank to stop their search for spiritual truth when they reach the limits of human reasoning and empirical evidence.

Perhaps the two camps of settlers could survive adequately without venturing beyond the limits of their respective riverbanks. The late Harvard paleontologist and gifted science writer Stephen Jay Gould saw value in keeping faith sequestered on one riverbank and science on another. His approach, first described in a 1997 essay called "Non-Overlapping Magisteria" for *Natural History* magazine, advocated a view of science and religion in which both domains spoke to their own issues without overlapping.[1] Science would address questions about how the universe works while religion would address questions of ultimate meaning and moral value. He found a way for the two camps to be at peace, but with limited dialogue.

I join Isaac Newton and the early settlers of Pittsburgh in the conviction that a richer life waits for those willing to construct a bridge. The settlers on the first riverbank can benefit when they consider a role for the life of the mind in the life of faith. When an expert in the Jewish law tested Jesus by asking him which commandment was the greatest one in the Law, Jesus replied, "'Love the Lord your God with all your heart and with all your soul and with all your mind.' This is the first and greatest commandment" (Mt 22:37-38). Heart, soul and mind—the whole person, both intellect and emotions, worshiping God! In his letter to Timothy, who was like a son to him, the apostle Paul counseled, "Do your best to present yourself to God as one approved, a worker who does not need to be ashamed and who correctly handles the word of truth" (2 Tim 2:15). Paul understood that preparation leads to sound teaching. He knew that proper study prevents aimless quarrels over peripheral issues. He knew that godly thinking guards against false doctrine. He wanted his son in the faith to be ready to gently instruct others so the gospel message would be carried forward to the next generation.

In Romans 10:2, Paul spoke of his concern for the Israelites, "For I can testify about them that they are zealous for God, but their zeal is not based on knowledge." He recognized that passion is not a substitute for truth. A strong belief can still be a wrong belief. He pointed out to the Romans that faith comes from hearing the Word of God. Learning mixed with faith brings life-changing results. The apostle Peter instructed believers to "be prepared to give an answer to everyone who asks you to give the reason for the hope that you have" (1 Pet 3:15). Like Paul, Peter understood the need for preparation and careful thinking.

A faith based in rational thought will protect the first group of settlers from foolish superstitions and dangerous false doctrine. Christians who disparage the role of reason in the life of faith become vulnerable to exploitation by unscrupulous religious leaders. They are more likely to become victims of spiritual abuse. Faith based primarily on emotions and experiences can easily crumble in the face of challenging circumstances, like a house with a foundation built on sand. A coherent worldview shaped by reasoning will help these settlers make God-honoring decisions, withstand adversity and intelligently communicate their beliefs to the world around them. In the process, they will begin to build a bridge to the settlers on the other side.

Those on the second riverbank appreciate the scientific method as a wonderful tool for understanding the natural world. With this tool, they avoid presumption and carefully test theories against reality. Yet many of the richest aspects of human existence are not measurable or understandable through the empirical scientific method although they are real and true. Consider the contributions of beauty, art, love, compassion and justice to human flourishing. If reliance on human reasoning excludes exploring these immaterial and abstract realities, the materialist risks living an impoverished life devoid of the knowledge beyond the reaches of a laboratory. The temptation, echoing Eve's choice in Eden, is to allow human reasoning to become the final authority on moral truth, rejecting an absolute standard set by God.

Humans living in the twenty-first century look on the understanding of humans from previous centuries with a sense of superiority. We view their limitations with quaint nostalgia. How could they comprehend our world with social media, instantaneous communication and countless medical advances? They lived out their entire lives without our more detailed scientific understanding of the world. Their limited human understanding was of some use, but a greater understanding was possible. Christians acknowledge that God, defined as the Creator of all, possesses an understanding far greater than ours. When he warns us not to lean on our own understanding, he is not condemning human reasoning. He is advising us of our limitations. He does not want us to despair when we view our circumstances with our narrow human perspective. Instead, he wants us to be encouraged by the knowledge that both our individual lives and the universe we inhabit contain beauty and purpose we have yet to uncover.

We must value our ability to think yet realize that the three pounds of quivering neurons processing information above our shoulders cannot fully understand all the mysteries of the universe. God does not ask us to abandon our limited understanding for blind faith. He simply desires that we do not become tethered by our inadequate knowledge when our faith in him can free our lives to soar to new heights.

FINDING SCIENCE EVERYWHERE

I suppose I always have appreciated special places that function as sanctuaries from the normal rush of everyday life. Long before I became a member of the Harvard Club, I enjoyed a different type of sanctuary as a child growing up in Pittsburgh. Phipps Conservatory and Botanical Gardens, a magnificent steel-and-glass Victorian greenhouse located in the city's Oakland neighborhood not far from the University of Pittsburgh, became a haven for me during school vacations and summers.

Inside the various greenhouse rooms, you could step into other lands without ever boarding a plane. Although his office was located in the South Hills of Pittsburgh, my father made frequent trips to Oakland to conduct research at the main branch of the Carnegie Library of Pittsburgh located just beyond the Cathedral of Learning on the University of Pittsburgh campus. While Oakland was an urban area, just a mile from the library a crystal palace of lush greenery awaited exploration at the entrance of Schenley Park. Whenever I came along with my father on his trips to Oakland, we would visit Phipps Conservatory together.

When we entered the Palm Court filled with thick foliage and towering palm trees, the air dripped with moisture. Moving through the South Conservatory with its water fountains and large center bed of seasonal flowers, we made our way to the Tropical Fruit and Spice Room to smell the living potpourri of cinnamon, allspice and citrus growing in the tropical climate. Next on the agenda was the Orchid Room, with a stream containing goldfish running through the center of an exhibit of orchids hanging from trees in a natural setting.

The highlight of each trip for both of us was the Desert Room. This area contained cacti and succulents that grew in arid climates very different from the humid continental climate zone in Pittsburgh. The philanthropist Henry Phipps Jr., for whom the conservatory is named, added the Desert Room (then called the Cacti House) in 1902 so that the people of Pittsburgh could observe these plants outside the pages of a book. In an era before airplane travel, he created an opportunity for an average person to see a cactus in person and connect to faraway lands. The cacti flourished under the protective glass and Pittsburgh sun, growing to enormous height.

On one of our trips, as we turned the bend on the serpentine path leading through the room, I saw a large plant that looked like an over-grown *Aloe vera* with gray-green leaves. "Hey, Dad, what is that plant?"

"That's a century plant. It blooms once every hundred years, then it dies." I learned years later that the plant's name was an exaggeration. The plant, *Agave americana*, took somewhere between ten and seventy years to bloom, depending on the climate.

"Did you ever see one bloom?"

"No, but this plant was here before you were born. I'm not sure how old it is. Maybe we will both see it bloom when you are my age."

His age. My mind tried to project forward to a hazy future moment when we stood together observing the giant century plant in bloom.

Science lived unobtrusively within those glass walls built in 1893, taking a back seat to beauty. The Victorian greenhouses served up a feast for the senses and stimulated the imagination. Exhibits taught lessons about history, geography and culinary traditions. Wandering those gardens, your mind could move between reliving the past and dreaming of the future. The colors and textures of plants created a certain mood within each greenhouse room. Yet underneath each plant a small bronze plaque unveiled scientific information for those who cared to look more closely. Science was everywhere, but never in the way.

Phipps Conservatory shaped my view of science in connection to other disciplines. I learned to appreciate science as a tool to enrich different pursuits in life. Science had limits at the boundaries of other academic subjects, but the limitations did not diminish the value of science. Erwin Schrödinger, recipient of the 1933 Nobel Prize in Physics and one of the fathers of quantum mechanics, expressed his thoughts on the limits of science in these words:

I am very astonished that the scientific picture of the real world around me is very deficient. It gives a lot of factual information, puts all our experience in a magnificently consistent order, but it is ghastly silent about all and sundry that is really near to our heart, that really matters to us. It cannot tell us a word about red and blue, bitter and sweet, physical pain and physical delight; it knows nothing of beautiful and ugly, good or bad, God and eternity. Science sometimes pretends to answer questions in these domains, but the answers are very often so silly that we are not inclined to take them seriously.[2]

In other words, Schrödinger thought that while science explains the material universe very well, many aspects of the human experience do not lend themselves to scientific inquiry. Although science can provide knowledge that informs decisions, science does not make moral judgments. Science may be able to explain why we perceive certain facial features as attractive or define the wavelengths that correspond to different colors, but science does not make aesthetic judgments. Finally, when operating properly within its sphere of influence, science does not draw conclusions about the supernatural.

Peter Medawar, the 1960 recipient of the Nobel Prize in Physiology or Medicine and a British immunologist who paved the way for organ transplantation, held views on the limits of science similar to those of Schrödinger. Medawar stated in his book *The Limits of Science,* "That there is indeed a limit upon science is made very likely by the existence of questions that science cannot answer, and that no conceivable advance of science would empower it to answer. . . . I have in mind such questions as: How did everything begin? What are we all here for? What is the point of living?" He did not feel that the inability to arrive at a scientific answer invalidated the question. When science had no response to an inquiry, he offered this advice: "We must turn to imaginative literature and religion for suitable answers!"[3]

Science could help me understand the biochemical processes that make a plant bloom and help the staff of the conservatory care for the plants in the garden. While science would become a vital part of my future, science could not predict that future. Sometimes when a flower opens, botany gives way to poetry, enriching our lives in a way that science alone cannot comprehend.

On my last visit to Pittsburgh eight weeks before my father died, my two daughters and I took him to visit Phipps Conservatory. We all made the journey together to the Desert Room and found the giant century plant, now nearly nine feet in diameter and eighteen feet high. I took a photo of my oldest daughter in front of the plant, which appeared unchanged from my childhood memories except for its increased size.

"Mom," said my six-year-old firstborn daughter, Allison, "did you ever see a century plant bloom?"

"No, but this plant was here before you were born. It was here even before I was born. Someday soon, we'll see it bloom."

"Grandpa, did you ever see one bloom?"

"No, I have come here all my life, but I am still waiting to see it."

Fifteen months after the end of my father's earthly journey, blossoming time came for the American century plant of his youth and my childhood. The stalk, resembling a giant asparagus, surged upward from the base of the plant at a rate of twelve inches of growth a day in March 2010, expending the energy stored over a lifetime for a final burst of glory. Beside the rosette of leaves, the conservatory placed a bronze plaque with the instruction, "Look up!" Within a month, the stalk brushed the roof of the Desert Room. Staff at the conservatory removed the glass pane directly over the century plant, and the stalk left the confines of the Victorian greenhouse. No longer in an artificial desert, the stalk experienced an early springtime frost and the moist air and whipping winds of Pittsburgh storms. Yet, determined to complete its mission, the stalk grew unfazed until it towered twelve feet above the greenhouse roof. At one point, high winds caused the stalk to snap, but bandaged with duct tape and secured by a splint and ropes, the stalk branched out under the summer sun. Soon tubular yellow flowers covered the branches, welcoming local birds to roost on an exotic perch. Destiny fulfilled, the stalk collapsed, and the leaves withered as small offshoots called pups grew at the base, ready to start the cycle once more.

Science is a part of our lives, even if we never set foot inside a laboratory. Scientific discoveries shape our environments, spark our imaginations and provide metaphors for life experiences. The blooming century plant underscored the reality of human limitations and the frailty of life, along with the role of persistence in fulfilling our destinies and creating a legacy for the next generation. Some dreams take more than one lifetime to come to fruition.

Discovering Inherent Uncertainty

We look to science to help us understand the cause of current events and increase our ability to plan for future events. The public expects science to deliver discoveries that provide increasingly precise answers about our world. Yet some scientific discoveries suggest inherent limits to scientific knowledge. These boundaries are not soft shorelines that time and research can erode but permanent limitations to the explanatory power of science. Werner Heisenberg, one of the greatest theoretical physicists of the twentieth century and a distinguished classical pianist, gave us one of these known unknowables of science. The Heisenberg uncertainty principle states that you cannot know both the precise position and the momentum of an atomic particle at any given time.[4] With these two paired physical properties of a particle, the more precisely you measure the one property, the less precisely you can determine the other. This insight changed the way we view our ability to predict the future through science, at least on the atomic level. In Newton's classical model, if you knew the present properties of an object, you could determine its future motion. This model still holds for everyday objects such as a car speeding down the highway or a baseball bouncing off the left field wall. However, once you reach the atomic level, quantum mechanics takes over. On this level, a scientist cannot calculate the precise future motion of a particle, only a range of possibilities. The limit is not our ability to construct better scientific instruments but the very nature of the relationship between paired physical properties such as position and momentum. Thus, Werner Heisenberg's discovery dashed the hope that time, work and sufficiently powerful calculations can resolve all the unknowns in the universe.

Another example of a scientific discovery that suggests inherent limits to scientific knowledge is chaos theory, popularized as the "butterfly effect." The butterfly effect is a simple insight first extracted from the complex science of meteorology by Edward Lorenz at the Massachusetts Institute of Technology in 1961. Lorenz, a meteorology professor at MIT, built a mathematical model of air movement in the atmosphere as a means of predicting weather patterns. His model used twelve variables, representing measurements such as temperature and wind speed, whose values over time could be plotted as lines on a graph. One winter day, he entered some numbers into a computer program simulating weather patterns according to this model and walked out of his office to get a cup of coffee while the computer processed the calculations. He was repeating a simulation he had run earlier and chose to round off one of the twelve variables representing an atmospheric condition from 0.506127 to 0.506. When he returned, he found that this tiny alteration drastically transformed the entire pattern his computer program generated for a long-term weather forecast covering the next two months. From this observation, he concluded that small changes can create large consequences. He explained this insight in his 1972 paper, "Predictability: Does the Flap of a Butterfly's Wings in Brazil Set Off a Tornado in Texas?"[5]

His paper described both a practical limit for weather predictions and a philosophical limit for the explanatory powers of science. In complex, nonlinear systems, a small change in input can produce a large change in output. This sensitive dependence on initial conditions means weather predictions more than a week in advance will always be fairly inaccurate. The lesson of the butterfly effect is that our world will remain fundamentally unpredictable because tiny differences in our scientific measurements make too big a difference in the final answer when we try to project outcomes in complex, nonlinear systems.

The philosophical limit described by Lorenz is that chaos prevents us from knowing which butterfly caused the tornado. A small effect such as the flap of a butterfly's wings might have set off a tornado-producing change in atmospheric conditions, but we cannot tell if the butterfly was in Brazil or Boston. Everything happens for a reason, but science may be unable to determine an exact cause for an event. Scientists chasing butterflies after the tornado cannot be sure the butterfly captured in their net is truly the one that started the storm.

What factors and influences in your life have brought you to your current circumstances? You might answer this question by pointing to certain milestone events or crucial decisions you made along your journey, such as the choice of an educational focus, a first job, encouragement from a parent or guidance from a mentor. Maybe certain difficulties or challenges shaped your path. Your inborn talents and acquired skills probably contributed to your direction in life. Which butterfly? Was it several butterflies? Or did the many butterflies, fluttering in swirling paths that intersected, each contribute in vital yet untraceable ways?

Known unknowables of science should introduce a measure of humility to our quest for knowledge without lessening the importance of science. Human reason is a powerful tool for learning about the natural world. However, human reason has limitations. Those who shun the life of the mind as incompatible with faith must remember that ideas are important. Ideas change the way we live our daily lives. Just as a basic understanding of the cell cycle gives rise to new targets for cancer treatment, theology informs ministry practices, bioethics makes bedside decisions and philosophy guides business practices. Loving God with all our hearts, all our souls and all our minds means building a bridge between faith and reason.

At times, we also must build a bridge over the gap between our expectations and our experiences. Some doubts that arise in our minds start in our hearts. When life experiences bring disappointment and disillusionment, we need to investigate and challenge our doubts instead of ignoring them. Doubts are a necessary part of the practice of science. The scientific method requires exploring doubts and formulating new questions based on those doubts. Doubts can carry important truths in life as well as science. Yet doubts that help you solve problems are very different from doubts that tear down your confidence or destroy your faith. Building bridges means daring to ask the questions while having faith to find the answers. In so doing, you glorify the God who created you to think.

2

INTERPLAY OF INFLUENCES

All truly wise thoughts have been thought already
thousands of times; but to make them truly ours,
we must think them over again honestly,
till they take root in our personal experience.

JOHANN WOLFGANG VON GOETHE

And without faith it is impossible to please God,
because anyone who comes to him must believe that he exists
and that he rewards those who earnestly seek him.

HEBREWS 11:6

MOST OF A GRADUATE STUDENT'S LIFE is spent in classrooms, libraries and laboratories. Quiet moments sitting before a fireplace in luxurious surroundings come rarely. I spent the majority of my days learning facts and gaining experience on the path to becoming a professional in my chosen field. Graduate education requires learning new ways of thinking, developing a different perspective and acquiring certain ideas common to one's academic discipline.

Both inside and outside the university setting, a variety of factors shape our beliefs. Our exposure to information, our emotional response to events and our relationships with important people in our lives mold us into the people we become. Students come to a university campus with a wide range of worldviews based on the location of their hometown, the political and religious beliefs of their parents, and their early experiences. In addition, shared experiences shape each generation. Every August since 1998, Beloit College releases the Beloit College Mindset List,[1] which examines the cultural touchstones that shape the lives of incoming college freshmen. At any age, recognizing the interplay of influences in your life can help you understand why you believe what you do and why you reject certain beliefs. This insight can help you examine your doubts from a fresh perspective.

Faith, facts and experience contribute to how we perceive the world. While we might be tempted to relegate faith to the domain of religion and facts to the domain of science, embracing Christianity requires a pursuit of knowledge, and great scientific discoveries often require a leap of insight not unlike faith. Experience gives meaning to the facts we discover and the faith we embrace, making the abstract become personal.

Beliefs start with observations we make through our five senses. Yet our five senses fail to perceive certain aspects of our world. For example, our naked eyes cannot see infrared and ultraviolet light, two bandwidths of the electromagnetic spectrum. However, science and technology expand our ability to perceive objective reality through instrumentation such as spectrometers and UV radiometers. We see very small objects through microscopes and very distant objects through telescopes. Through observation, we learn truths we label as facts. In science, a fact is a provable concept, an objective and verifiable observation. No matter who performs a scientific experiment, the scientific facts should remain unchanged. For example, the temperature of a room measures the same degrees Fahrenheit no matter who checks the thermometer.

In everyday life, facts filter through our subjective experience. We create our models of objective reality from selective data, meaning we pay more attention to certain information and store, retain and recall it more efficiently than other information. This effect, known as a cognitive bias, shapes our beliefs without our awareness. For example, we learn from a young age the importance of making a good impression when meeting someone for the first time. This piece of life wisdom acknowledges the significance of the primacy effect, which causes a person to assume that the first piece of evidence for a belief is the most important and worth remembering. The firmness of a job candidate's handshake may not be as important as his tendency to procrastinate until days before a project's deadline, but the interviewer will remember his confident handshake and learn about the procrastination months after hiring him.

If you have ever experienced frustration trying to persuade someone to change his or her mind, you may have encountered the confirmation bias. This cognitive bias recognizes the tendency for people to favor information that confirms their existing beliefs. As a result of this bias, people become overconfident in their own thinking and resistant to new discoveries.

The way we understand our world stems not only from facts and personal experience but also from the influence of significant people in our lives. We often more readily accept information presented by authority figures such as parents, pastors, teachers and coaches. The opinions of our friends, colleagues and other peers can shape our beliefs as well. Some people rely more heavily on the opinions of others while others trust their own reasoning and experience to a higher degree. Of course, rebelling against the beliefs of those in authority or against the prevailing beliefs of our peer group is just the influence of others working in reverse. By becoming more aware of how people in our lives affect our beliefs, we can examine our beliefs with greater honesty.

Richard Dawkins, the British evolutionary biologist and popular author, considers faith "the great cop-out, the great excuse to evade the need to think and evaluate evidence. Faith is belief in spite of, even perhaps because of, the lack of evidence."[2] To Dawkins, faith occurs in a void separate from facts and experience. Alister McGrath, the British Irish theologian and molecular biophysicist, takes a different view of faith. He believes "faith is not something that goes against the evidence, it goes beyond it. The evidence is saying to us, 'There is another country. There is something beyond mere reason.'" To McGrath, faith completes the picture drawn by facts and experience.

C. S. Lewis saw faith in Christianity not only as reasonable but also as the key to understanding everything else about human experience. In his words, "I believe in Christianity as I believe that the sun has risen—not only because I see it, but because by it, I see everything else."[3] Faith illuminates facts and experience for C. S. Lewis. The noted Anglican theologian W. H. Griffith Thomas (1861–1924) thought faith affected "the whole of man's nature. It commences with the conviction of the mind based on adequate evidence; it continues in the confidence of the heart or emotions based on conviction, and it is crowned in the consent of the will, by means of which the conviction and confidence are expressed in conduct."[4] Thomas sees faith not only helping us understand life, but also changing the way we live our life.

COMPASSION AND RESEARCH

I think faith affects life choices in the same way a ride in the main elevator at a cancer institute impacted my early years as a scientific researcher. At Penn State University, I worked in laboratories housed either in classroom buildings or in buildings dedicated completely to research. In this environment, I saw only professors, staff, students and the occasional scientific sales representative during the course of my day. This atmosphere led to an academic focus for my scientific research. While I thought about the potential beneficiaries of my research, those individuals existed in theory rather than practice.

At Harvard Medical School, I discovered many research laboratories located in hospitals. As a new graduate student, I needed to complete two or three laboratory rotations before choosing a lab for my thesis research. During a laboratory rotation, a student would work on a short research project for several months in a lab in order to see if both the research topic and the people in the lab were a good fit for the student's interests. I chose to do my first rotation in the lab of a pediatric oncologist in the Dana-Farber Cancer Institute. The lab was on the sixteenth floor of the hospital, which had some floors dedicated to patient care and others to research labs. You could look out the large windows of the lab and see portions of the Boston skyline. The panoramic view added to my excitement for this new research opportunity. Of course, once I started a new experiment I rarely looked up from the bench.

Each day I would ride one of the two elevators in the main lobby to the top of the building to go to my new lab. As part of my orientation as a new researcher at the institute, I learned two rules governing my use of the lobby elevators. The first rule was to remove my white lab gloves before entering the elevator. The second was to refrain from discussing research or patient matters while on the elevator. The management of the institute created both rules to protect the patients and their family members who rode the elevators to the treatment floors of the hospital.

Those lobby elevators put my research into context. One beautiful Saturday afternoon when I would have preferred to go on a long walk in Larz Anderson Park with my husband instead of spending the time setting up an experiment for the following week, a woman wearing a plum and lilac headscarf followed me onto the elevator. After exchanging a quick hello and a smile, we rode together in silence until she reached the floor housing the clinic. The ride from her floor to the top of the building took only a few seconds, yet provided sufficient time to renew my focus. I was young. I was healthy. My hair cascaded down past my shoulders. I came to the cancer institute to pursue a dream and prepare for the future. She came to the cancer institute to fight for a future.

As I pulled my hair back into a ponytail and put on my lab coat, I realized the woman probably had some better place to be that Saturday afternoon. Maybe she wanted to attend her son's soccer game or go shopping with her daughter. Maybe she wanted to sit outside and read a good book or get ready to go out to dinner with her husband. Instead, she had no choice but to come to the clinic. I came to the hospital by choice. I could leave at any point.

I placed a stack of tissue culture dishes in the sterile hood and put a bottle of media in a warm water bath. My experiment would never benefit the woman I met in the elevator. Yet, my experiment belonged in the long chain of knowledge from basic research to clinical treatment. In ten or twenty years, a different woman might step out of the elevator to receive a better treatment with fewer side effects thanks to insights from basic research occurring in labs like mine. I decided to dedicate my work that afternoon to the woman with the purple and lilac headscarf.

Working at a cancer institute committed to patient care as well as scientific advancement taught me how compassion can drive achievement. Of course, compassion does not affect the experimental design or the collection of data. However, compassion changes the hearts of researchers, helping them start earlier, work harder and persevere longer. In the same way, faith changes how we view our experiences, while leaving the facts unchanged. The Bible reminds us God "causes his sun to rise on the evil and the good, and sends rain on the righteous and the unrighteous" (Mt 5:45). In other words, his provision of sun and rain necessary for the growth of crops is the same for both those who have faith and those who do not. The experience is the same for both the believer and the unbeliever, but by faith the believer expresses gratitude for favorable weather. In times of unfavorable weather, faith supplies the believer with the patience to persevere and hope for a better tomorrow.

Faith can transform a person even when circumstances remain unchanged. Of course, the change in a person can be experienced by others and becomes empirical evidence notable by others, intertwining the relationship between faith, facts and experience. Consider how the apostle Peter changed on the day of Pentecost. After Jesus was arrested and taken before the Sanhedrin (a judicial council of Jewish religious leaders), Peter denied three times that he knew Jesus (Mt 26:57-75; Mk 14:53-72; Lk 22:54-62; Jn 18:15-27). He lacked the courage to stand up for what he believed, even before a servant girl. On the day of Pentecost, we see a very different Peter (Acts 2:14-41). He stood up, raised his voice and addressed a large crowd containing mockers. He spoke confidently and called the people to repentance. He warned the people, and three thousand of them accepted his message. The Peter on the day of Pentecost possessed courage and conviction. He had seen the risen Christ (Jn 21:15-23) and experienced the infilling of the Holy Spirit (Acts 2:4).

The transformation of Peter was an observable phenomenon, a type of empirical evidence. Peter had a personal experience he explained through his faith in the Scriptures. The responses of three thousand people to Peter's message are data about their decisions of faith. They chose to have faith not because of a lack of evidence or in spite of evidence, as Richard Dawkins describes, but as a result of both evidence and an experience. In keeping with Alister McGrath's view of faith, some people first thought the evidence on the day of Pentecost pointed to the disciples being drunk before they accepted Peter's explanation of the work of the Holy Spirit. They moved beyond a natural explanation to a supernatural explanation.

Peter quoted the prophet Joel (Acts 2:17-21; Joel 2:28-32) to give a context for the experience of Pentecost, and then he explained the purpose of Jesus' life, death and resurrection in the context of David's words from Psalms 16 and 110. Peter's explanation provided a framework for the people to understand recent events. As C. S. Lewis would affirm, Peter's description of the central message of Christianity became the light by which the people saw everything else. The people who made a decision to accept the message of Christianity that day experienced life change. "They devoted themselves to the apostles' teaching and to fellowship, to the breaking of bread and to prayer" (Acts 2:42). The people went through the process described by W. H. Griffith Thomas. Peter's sermon brought conviction of the mind based on adequate evidence, which continued in the confidence of the heart and the consent of the will to produce changed conduct. Their hearts changed and their lives changed by believing the message supported by evidence yet only accessible by faith.

ECHOES OF A PRAYER

I chose to remain at the Dana-Farber Cancer Institute to complete my second rotation, and I stayed in this lab for my doctoral research. The intricate mechanisms of the cell cycle responsible for controlling cell growth became the focus for my work. As a child, I enjoyed arranging dominoes in winding lines that ran over ramps and formed intricate patterns. Pushing over the first domino started a cascade of falling dominoes, which rippled over the ramps and through the pattern to the end of the line. Similarly, in a cell, a signal at the surface membrane starts a cascade that transmits information to the nucleus deep in the center of the cell, initiating the duplication of the cell's genetic blueprint in preparation for the division of one cell into two. I enjoyed the challenge of unraveling the cascading events that controlled cell growth, a process tightly regulated in normal cells but defective in cancer cells. In order to better understand the place of certain cellular dominoes in the chain of signaling events, I would read the scientific literature to keep current with the discoveries of other scientists trying to solve the same puzzle. One morning while reading a journal article referring to signaling events in lung cancer cells, I remembered my maternal grandfather, Andy.

Nearly forty years ago, he walked his youngest daughter, my mother, down the aisle in a big, beautiful church wedding. He had six children, four of whom were girls, and my mother was the baby of the family. In those days, the Catholic Church would not allow a church wedding unless you married another Catholic. My mother's three older sisters did not marry within the Catholic faith, thrice dashing my grandfather's dream of walking a daughter down the aisle.

From his early teens onward, Andy's life revolved around working hard to provide for his family. After his own father came home blind from an accident in the steel mills of Pittsburgh, Andy became the provider in his father's place, a role that only intensified when he married young and became a father himself. In his early fifties, weary after a long day driving a bread delivery truck, he would sit at the dinner table enjoying a piece of my grandmother's homemade pie and say, "I just want to live long enough to see all my children raised and married." On June 27, 1953, Andy met his goal when my mother married my father, a graduate of Central Catholic High School, a prestigious high school for boys located near Carnegie Mellon University in Pittsburgh. A few days after the wedding, my father, drafted into the army during the Korean War, headed for Germany, and my mother continued to live with her parents. As if by a self-fulfilling prophecy, soon after my father arrived overseas the doctors informed my grandmother, aunts, uncles and mother that my grandfather had lung cancer. Doctors in that era avoided telling the patient the bad news. As his symptoms worsened, Andy could no longer drive his delivery truck. He knew this illness was unlike any other he had ever experienced, and he pressed family members to tell him the truth about his diagnosis.

Once he knew the truth, he spent his remaining days pacing from one end of his small two-bedroom house to the other to cope with the physical pain he felt, praying that none of his children would ever suffer from lung cancer. He also prayed doctors would make progress in treating cancer in the future, for he knew the doctors were failing to cure his own disease. A strong and determined man, Andy found that pacing suited his nature much better than lying down in bed, even when he needed to hold on to furniture for support.

When his time came, Andy took one final trip through the rooms of the house where he raised six children, traveling from the master bedroom in the back of the house down the hallway past my mother's bedroom to the kitchen, and then through the dining room to the front parlor. Running out of breath on his journey from the parlor back to the master bedroom, he sat down and called to my grandmother, "Mary, I'm dying." Frightened, my grandmother ran next door to her sister's house to get help, and my mother rushed to her father's side.

"Dad, I'm here with you until Mum returns. Tell me what you need."

Although my grandmother returned quickly with her sister, the minutes felt like hours to my twenty-two-year-old mother, who mustered physical and emotional strength beyond her capabilities to keep my grandfather from falling before and after he took his last breath.

The three women carried my grandfather back to the master bedroom and closed his eyes with two pennies. The moment marked a turning point in my mother's life. My grandfather had provided my mother with a sense of security and direction now forever lost. With her husband in Germany and her mother overwhelmed by grief, she felt the weight of responsibility for the family and became a stronger, more independent woman. When my father returned more than a year later from his overseas army duty, he found a very different woman from the one he had married. Sitting around the dinner table growing up, I heard both my parents tell stories about those two years with such vivid details that their memories from the early 1950s feel like my own.

As I read the scientific article on lung cancer cells many years later, I wondered whether my presence in this cancer institute was somehow an answer to one of my grandfather's prayers. While only God knows the correct response to that question, the echoes of my grandfather's prayers touched my heart although he died more than a decade before my birth. As with any question of answered prayer, we can reach for a supernatural explanation or seek a natural cause.

People of faith often ask me how doctors view cancer remissions that patients claim were miraculous answers to prayer. Most doctors will view such an event as a statistical outlier, a rare but possible occurrence. Others will consider natural explanations such as a hormonal or immune response. A few may make room for a faith-based reason. Patients who believe they experienced a supernatural healing should not disparage doctors who seek a naturalistic explanation. Those doctors are doing their jobs. If a natural mechanism is at work to provide a cure for a disease, everyone benefits when a doctor uncovers it.

Of course, the evidence of God's hand at work in a person's circumstances can stir faith in the hearts of those who witness the answered prayer. The Bible tells us that "without faith it is impossible to please God, because anyone who comes to him must believe that he exists and that he rewards those who earnestly seek him" (Heb 11:6). While evidence and experience can point us to God, the need for a final step of faith remains. According to the Bible, we please God when we have faith in his existence and in his character. Seeking God requires action and sincerity. The act of believing is important, but so is the veracity of the belief itself. A strong belief can be a wrong belief, for passion can exist separate from accuracy. Teaching that sounds good can contain error, for persuasion works even for lies. In 1 Corinthians 2:4-5, the apostle Paul tells the Corinthian believers, "My message and my preaching were not with wise and persuasive words, but with a demonstration of the Spirit's power, so that your faith might not rest on human wisdom, but on God's power." Paul acknowledged the place for facts and experience in verifying teaching because he understood the importance of substance over style. Evidence of God at work in people's lives backed up the truth of Paul's message. Spiritual truth must be rooted in more than a claim of revelation, for any religious teacher can make such a claim. The strength of the Bible is the watermark of verifiable truth on the pages of revealed truth. For example, the prophecies within the Bible are open to empirical verification. In addition, the effect of biblical teachings on individual lives and on society is open to investigation. These elements of truth help us to determine the reasonableness of our faith without negating the need for faith itself. We take the final step of faith toward the light of revelation, not into the darkness of ignorance.

The possibility of my grandfather's prayers being answered in the life of a granddaughter yet unborn raises the question of what time frame is appropriate for measuring an answer to prayer. Like a prophecy that looks to the future, a prayer can reach beyond one lifetime. Whether or not the prayer gets the credit, the answer comes. The moment may occur at a time unknown to the one who prayed, although that person saw the answer by faith long before the answer came. Faith comes from a person's confidence in God's desire and ability to hear and answer prayer as described in 1 John 5:14-15: "This is the confidence we have in approaching God: that if we ask anything according to his will, he hears us. And if we know that he hears us—whatever we ask—we know that we have what we asked of him." Although the person may not live to see evidence of the answer of a particular prayer, someday that evidence will exist. Facts and experience lead to faith, and faith produces facts and experience.

Yet, like the biblical heroes of faith described in Hebrews 11, a person may die without seeing the awaited answer to a prayer. "All these people were still living by faith when they died. They did not receive the things promised; they only saw them and welcomed them from a distance" (Heb 11:13). Abraham believed God's promise that his descendants would be as numerous as the stars in the sky and as countless as the sand on the seashore. While he lived to become the father of Isaac, he saw the multiplication of his heirs only by faith. The fulfillment of this promise would take generations, and Abraham faced the limitations of time.

To many people, prayer is a cry for help spoken in an emergency. We pray for safety in a storm, healing from an illness or peace in a crisis. Even when we pray with a little more planning, our prayers tend to center on current needs and a short-term horizon: "Please help my friend find a job." "Protect our missionaries as they travel." "Bless our outreach next month."

Of course, Jesus modeled praying for daily needs with the words "give us today our daily bread" (Mt 6:11). A large component of faith is the willingness to maintain an attitude of dependence on God for every aspect of life. However, sometimes through faith we pray prayers of "your kingdom come, your will be done, on earth as it is in heaven" (Mt 6:10). These prayers stretch across the years necessary to realize larger goals, for no kingdom comes in an instant. My grandfather prayed this kind of prayer, and so did Abraham.

I closed the research journal and thought about my grandfather's determination. With only an eighth-grade education, he earned enough money to send his younger brother to college and then put food on the table for his six children, hanging on to his health until his youngest daughter found a husband. He put the needs of others first his entire life, including the final weeks spent in pain from terminal cancer. As his granddaughter, I shared his determination to make progress against the disease that took his life. The tasks ahead of me seemed less daunting when I heard the echoes of my grandfather's prayers.

THE SIGNIFICANCE OF BACKGROUND

After taking a year and a half of courses and choosing a thesis lab, I was ready to clear the first major hurdle of academic life, the qualifying exam. In some graduate programs, students take a written exam that tests the depth and breadth of their knowledge within their chosen field of study. At Harvard Medical School, the qualifying exam takes a practical approach to testing a student's readiness for the life of a researcher. To obtain funding for research, the head of the laboratory, called the principal investigator, prepares grants explaining the rationale for future research plans. These grant applications also function to guide the design of experiments by all the members of the lab. The qualifying exam for my program at Harvard reflected this process, giving students an opportunity to write a research plan and present it before a committee of professors.

While the qualifying exam felt like a formidable challenge, I thought the time I would need to spend in preparation would be meaningful. Any student who reaches the second year of graduate school is an expert in preparing for tests. However, graduate school is not about memorizing facts, but about analyzing facts. A good researcher can retrieve a forgotten fact or helpful equation from a journal or textbook without much trouble. The challenge for a researcher is handling the facts. Which facts carry the most weight? Are certain facts irrelevant to the question at hand? Which facts are related to other facts? Can I combine certain facts to create a story? Can these facts help me discover new facts?

I would have been happy to pull out my old notebooks and review facts about molecular biology, biochemistry, genetics, microbiology and immunology in preparation for a written test. However, the qualifying exam gave me the opportunity to think like a researcher. What scientific problem did I want to solve? What experiments must I conduct to solve this problem? What information must I gather before I designed my first experiment? How should I present this information in my presentation?

As I wrote my research proposal on finding potential regulators of the tumor suppressor p53, the most frequently altered gene in human cancers,[5] I learned one of the key lessons of the qualifying exam: past knowledge shapes future direction. After describing the specific aims or goals of your planned research, the first required section of the proposal is "Background and Significance." Before you can move the frontier of scientific knowledge forward, you need to know all that has come before. The background to a research proposal involves a thorough search of the scientific literature to review the work of other researchers working on similar problems and topics. No one wants to pay for someone to rediscover knowledge already on the shelf in the medical library.

Of course, a researcher not only needs to know the background behind his proposed research; he also needs to know what information is significant for his future experiments. Great discoveries come from researchers able to discern the significant from the trivial. Sorting through information to find the important connections between seemingly unrelated facts is a vital skill for a scientist. Our ability to understand our background and its influence on our present decisions has value in life as well as in the laboratory.

A research proposal starts by examining the significance of background information, and then sets a researcher free to make creative future plans. A researcher is informed by the past, but not bound by the past. In the same way, once you understand how past influences have shaped your current beliefs, you are free to make a fresh decision for the future.

The U.S. Religious Landscape Survey by the Pew Forum on Religion and Public Life,[6] based on interviews with 35,000 Americans aged eighteen and older, determined that 28% of American adults have left the religion of their childhood for another religion or no religion at all. If you include a change in Protestant denominations, the percentage increases to 44% of adults who have added, dropped or switched a religious affiliation. Another way to look at those statistics is to conclude that the majority of Americans stick with the religious affiliation of their childhood, although many people are open to change. I suspect significant relationships and events in people's lives shape their views on spiritual matters more than they are aware.

When you examine your faith or lack of faith, what events can you identify that have led you to your current beliefs? What role has thinking played in your journey of faith or quest for truth? Do you rely heavily on your own reasoning? Do you tend to accept information presented by an authority or accepted by your circle of friends? Are feelings and experiences more important to you than facts and logical arguments? We all approach life in a unique way, integrating information and experiences based on our abilities, preferences, temperament and cultural conditioning.

While the location of your hometown and the beliefs of your parents may influence whether you are exposed to a faith such as Christianity, Christianity knows no geographical or socioeconomic boundaries. Jesus said, "Come to me, all you who are weary and burdened, and I will give you rest" (Mt 11:28). His invitation stands no matter the culture, the time period or the location. As Jesus explained

to the Jewish religious teacher Nicodemus, who came at night to seek
spiritual truth by talking with Jesus away from observation by the
other religious teachers, "For God so loved the world that he gave his
one and only Son, that whoever believes in him shall not perish but
have eternal life" (Jn 3:16). The Christian message is for the world,
open to anyone who believes.

Of course, while the Christian message is for the world, different
churches express that message in a myriad of ways. People's views
about church and the expressions of their faith often reflect their previous experiences. A person raised in a church environment heavy on
rules may seek a church with a looser structure that emphasizes grace.
Yet another person may desire to replicate his or her childhood church
experiences in adulthood by joining a church with a similar approach
to ministry. Distinguishing between the core message of Christianity
and the cultural preferences of our own church background can be the
key to greater cooperation between Christians.

Faith, facts and personal experience come together when a person
embraces Christianity. Knowledge of the historical facts of Christianity combines with a person's experience of peace and joy to form a
reasonable basis for belief. Yet belief in the provision of eternal life to
those who accept Jesus Christ as their Lord and Savior remains a
matter of faith. Knowledge without trust is meaningless for salvation,
although trust flows from knowledge.

The Christian apologist and philosophy professor J. P. Moreland
notes, "God maintains a delicate balance between keeping his existence sufficiently evident so people will know he's there and yet hiding
his presence enough so that people who want to choose to ignore him
can do it." Faith and reason come together, but reason can never replace the need for faith.

A graduate student taking the qualifying exam experiences the
moment when hope, facts and experience come together while quietly

pacing in the hallway as the three to five faculty members on the qualifying exam committee discuss the student's fate beyond the closed door of the conference room. This moment takes place about two hours after the start of the graduate student's twenty-five-minute talk about proposed research aims. Of course, the talk lasts much longer than the planned twenty-five minutes because professors interrupt the presentation after every few slides to ask penetrating questions. If the professors do a good job, they will find a question that exposes gaps in the graduate student's background knowledge or flaws in the design of the proposed experiments. When the professors exhaust their supply of questions, the chair of the qualifying exam committee will ask the student to step outside the room while the professors discuss the student's performance.

Once the committee agrees on the student's fate, the chairman will invite the student back into the room to award the student a pass, fail or conditional pass. A conditional pass means the student needs to make certain changes to the research proposal before passing the exam. A student cannot submit a dissertation proposal, the first step toward completion of a doctoral thesis, until passing the qualifying exam. Most students do not fail, so the real concern of a student waiting in the hallway is whether he will walk back into his lab after the exam with his head held high celebrating a pass or trudge along saddled with the extra work and touch of academic dishonor that comes with a conditional pass.

The sequence of talk, questions and wait in the hallway begins a ritual the student will experience many times during a graduate research career, starting with the qualifying exam and culminating with the thesis defense, which marks the end of a student's doctoral studies. I spent about five minutes in the hallway after my qualifying exam before learning I received a clear pass. I had done a thorough job preparing the facts, which led to the experience of a wonderful celebratory party with cake and tea in my research lab, and a strengthening of my faith in the call on my life to become a scientist.

This event in my journey as a researcher was a hurdle I needed to surmount, similar to the hurdles we must overcome on our journey of faith. My knowledge of the facts behind the presentation remained unchanged before and after the exam, but my personal experience of joy and celebration led me to feel this moment was confirmation of my calling, despite any doubts I had in the months leading up to this event.

Bringing faith and facts together and allowing them to take root in our personal experience, as the German writer Goethe described, helps us make our beliefs and knowledge our own. When we recognize the interplay of influences shaping our worldview, we gain the ability to adjust our thinking, update it and discover new truths. We become better equipped to question doubts arising from our background, our cognitive biases, and the positive and negative influences of people in our lives. We can untangle our decisions about our beliefs from the legacies left by others and make new choices if necessary. In many cases, we may choose to honor and continue the heritage we examine, but we will be making the choice afresh and taking personal responsibility for the faith we decide to embrace and the doubts we cast aside.

3

DISCERNMENT REQUIRES DOUBTS

*Discernment is not a matter of simply
telling the difference between right and wrong;
rather, it is telling the difference between
right and almost right.*

CHARLES HADDON SPURGEON

*Test [everything]; hold on to what is good,
reject every kind of evil.*

1 THESSALONIANS 5:21-22

TWENTY-SEVEN MILES BEYOND the shore of Cape Cod, I stepped off a ferry into the damp, salty air of an April afternoon on Nantucket Island. Stretched in front of me along the wharf I found an array of curious shops setting the tone for my short escape from Boston into a haven belonging to another time.

"Watermelonade? Not sure what it is, but it seems worth a try."

Past the art galleries and gift shops, but before the bicycle rental shop, an ice cream and juice stand offered novel choices of refreshment, including watermelonade. While the temperature was in the low sixties, the long ferry ride from Hyannis to Steamship Wharf left me both thirsty and ready for a small culinary adventure. Sipping on the watermelonade, my husband and I pulled our luggage along the cobblestone street on our way to the bed and breakfast where we were staying. Beneath the dreary gray sky, cheerful yellow splashes of daffodils in window boxes, gardens and vases in shop windows promised spring sunshine.

I came to Nantucket seeking sunshine not only to provide a restful vacation but also to bring clarity to the direction of my research. Doubts filled my mind, but these doubts were the beneficial doubts that produce discernment. Red flags of caution may be cause for alarm, but they are a gift to keep us moving in a productive direction. Surrounded by the charm of another century, I hoped the increased objectivity that came from being miles away from my lab bench would help me resolve which of two directions to pursue in my doctorate research after two years of exploratory work on two projects. Entering the bed and breakfast in time for tea, I enjoyed meeting the other guests over clotted cream and scones, forgetting graduate school for the rest of the day.

ENCOUNTERING BENEFICIAL DOUBTS

We often view doubts as those black clouds that spoil the blue skies of faith. However, not all doubts are bad. While you can pray over every doubt, not every doubt should be prayed away. René Descartes's doubting helped him reason his way to God. Descartes, the father of analytical geometry and of modern philosophy, questioned his doubts by applying human reasoning to the mathematical method, the process that students use to write proofs in a high school geometry class. He started with unquestioned premises or axioms, then deduced logically irrefutable conclusions. But how did he find such unquestioned premises in the midst of doubt?

Descartes's approach to this challenge is fascinating. He reasoned that the one thing of which he could be certain was his doubts. He wrote, "What is there, then, that can be esteemed to be true? Perhaps this only, that there is absolutely nothing certain." He reasoned that doubt is a negative form of thought. The more a person doubts, the more certain the person becomes that he is thinking and that he exists. In Descartes's own words, "Doubtless, then, I exist, since I am deceived; and, let him deceive me as he may, he can never bring it about that I am nothing, so long as I shall be conscious that I am something." Complete doubt would bring complete certainty that one was thinking. I doubt; therefore, I am thinking. But if one is thinking, then one must be a thinking thing. He wrote, "I am therefore, precisely speaking, only a thinking thing, that is, a mind *(mens sive animus)*, understanding, or reason, terms whose signification was before unknown to me. I am, however, a real thing, and really existent; but what thing? The answer was, a thinking thing." The unquestioned premise, which is beyond doubt, is that the doubter is a thinking being with a mind. In his own words, "I readily discover that there is nothing more easily or clearly apprehended than my own mind."

Descartes moves from his only point of certainty—that of the existence of his own mind—to prove the existence of God, a Being with a perfect mind. He reasons that his doubts prove that he is imperfect, for a lack in knowledge is an imperfection. Yet the only way he could realize that he is imperfect is to have knowledge of the perfect. Such knowledge of the perfect could not arise from his own imperfect mind, because only a perfect Mind (God) could serve as the origin of the idea of perfection. He concluded, "And the whole force of the argument of which I have here availed myself to establish the existence of God, consists in this, that I perceive I could not possibly be of such a nature as I am, and yet have in my mind the idea of a God, if God did not in reality exist—this same God, I say, whose idea is in my mind—that is, a being who possesses all those lofty perfections, of which the mind may have some slight conception, without, however, being able fully to comprehend them, and who is wholly superior to all defect [and has nothing that marks imperfection]: whence it is sufficiently manifest that he cannot be a deceiver, since it is a dictate of the natural light that all fraud and deception spring from some defect."[1]

While we might dismiss Descartes's proof of God's existence as based on reasoning from an earlier age, we must acknowledge that doubting served a useful purpose in Descartes's own spiritual journey. One reason you should question your doubts is to determine if your doubts carry important truth. The small, still voice of caution telling you to check once more before proceeding is born as a beneficial doubt. The warning not to trust the flattering words of a supposed friend starts as a doubt. The wisdom to close a successful business deal comes from separating the information and relationships worth trusting from those that deserve doubting.

Some doubts will clarify your faith and correct your thinking. Some doubts will rescue you from error and arrogance. Beneficial doubts will help you to be "as shrewd as snakes and as innocent as doves" (Mt 10:16). You may find that you need to let go of a narrow view of God's protection and blessing to make room for his sovereignty. You may need to accept that no is a valid answer to prayer. Your doubts may come to correct and expand your theology. Instead of your faith shrinking in response to a prayer that was not answered the way you hoped, your faith can enlarge to worship a sovereign God whose "ways [are] higher than your ways" (Is 55:9). In the process, you will learn that God has not abandoned you. He is present in the emergency room after the accident, on the walk down the office corridor after losing your job and in the heartache after a breakup.

Doubts may help you find a new way of living out your faith. You may discover that what you thought was a biblical approach to leadership was simply an ingrained church tradition. You may separate your cultural expectations from biblical principles to embrace new worship experiences, new avenues of service and a wider circle of friends. During seasons of doubting when you recognize you do not have all the answers, you may well be capable of the greatest spiritual growth. In your desert time of doubting, you can find the oasis or you can die of dehydration. How you handle your doubts makes the difference. Will you learn from your doubts, or will your doubts hinder your happiness?

The uncertainty that accompanies all doubts, even beneficial ones, often brings restlessness and momentary confusion. The next day after arriving on Nantucket Island, my research concerns percolated in the back of my mind while I went through the motions of enjoying my vacation. After breakfast, my husband and I made our way to the rental shop where you could obtain the preferred method of transportation on the island, a bike with a beautiful woven basket. No trip to Nantucket would be complete without a bike ride to the beach. We set our sights on Sciasconset Beach, better known as simply Sconset Beach, on the east end of the island. The seven-mile journey from the rental shop to the beach seemed to be the perfect length. The first part of the trip involved biking on cobblestone streets, a very jarring endeavor. However, most of the trip entailed a serene ride on a paved two-way bike path.

The moment when we first experience doubts can feel as jolting as biking on cobblestone streets. We experience discordance between our current way of thinking and the data amassing to contradict it. Scholars in the field of education recognize that these experiences that create cognitive dissonance can be transformative, triggering life change and aiding the learning process.[2] Sometimes we need to ignore our doubts and keep plowing ahead. However, when the information that opposes our present approach begins to reach a certain critical mass, wisdom dictates we pause to ask discerning questions. Are there important details I have overlooked? Is wishful thinking clouding my judgment? Who can provide wise counsel or a second opinion on this matter? A traveler hoping to reach a destination in a reasonable amount of time knows to consult a map or ask for directions. Just as a wrong turn on one of the Nantucket streets early in my bike ride could have sent me far away from my desired direction, a wrong choice in life can keep you from reaching your goals. A growing sense that something is not right can help you correct your course with minimal loss.

Doubts can even protect your faith by alerting you to false teaching or unhealthy situations. If something is bothering you, pause and reflect to resolve your doubts. You may find that you are on course after all, or you may save yourself future pain by stepping back from a negative situation to assess the biblical perspective on your experience. Consider the possibility that God is speaking to you through the warning bells of doubt.

My doubts during that April in Nantucket helped me realize that I needed to close down one avenue of research to focus on another. After two years of work, dropping a project that represented a serious investment of my time was not an easy choice. I found both projects fascinating, yet one project emerged with a clearer path to a good scientific story than the other. I needed to trust my instincts as a researcher and make the call. While my doubts involved a scientific question, the process illustrates the value of doubts in the exercise of discernment.

The heaviness I felt as I faced the decision reached beyond a scientific judgment call to my deepest concerns about balance in my life between work goals and personal goals. I looked forward to having a family, and I feared a prolonged graduate career might hinder that goal. While I knew several graduate students who stayed at the lab bench during their pregnancies, I did not want to expose my unborn baby to the chemicals and radioactivity I used in my research. I also knew myself too well. While I admired those students who balanced research and motherhood, I knew that I wanted to give my undivided focus to each of those pursuits.

A poor judgment call about my research direction had the power to derail so many other dreams in my life. I had a gut feeling about how to proceed, but my resolve waivered.

The steady breeze blowing in from the shoreline made pedaling the bike harder but also signaled my arrival at my destination. The white sand on Sconset Beach and the azure waters belonged completely to my husband and me, for no one else came to the beach on that chilly April day.

EXPERIENCING DISSONANCE

Once you have experienced the cognitive dissonance of mounting evidence to support a doubt, you often feel confusion. At this stage, seeking guidance is critical. Sometimes we need to let a problem rest a little while, forgoing an immediate answer in the service of finding the right answer. The Bible affirms the importance of seeking wisdom in the midst of uncertainty in James 1:5-8:

> If any of you lacks wisdom, you should ask God, who gives generously to all without finding fault, and it will be given to you. But when you ask, you must believe and not doubt, because the one who doubts is like a wave of the sea, blown and tossed by the wind. That person should not expect to receive anything from the Lord. Such a person is double-minded and unstable in all they do.

The doubts that lead a person to ask for wisdom are positive doubts. However, this biblical passage instructs us not to doubt God's goodness and willingness to provide an answer. A person who vacillates between trusting God for guidance and doubting God's willingness to provide is like a wave heading to the shoreline. One moment the wave swells mighty and powerful, ready to sweep away everything in its path. The next moment, the wave hits its nadir, drawing debris downward into a watery pit. The end result of energy and dissipation, hope and despair, is a lack of coherent forward motion. A person swinging from trust to wariness loses all spiritual momentum.

However, doubting our direction, our choices and our thinking can help keep us in touch with our humanity. Overconfident people who believe they have all the answers are like ships heading for shore without heeding the lighthouse. Discernment keeps a ship away from the shoals. The painful part of discernment is admitting you are wrong in order to correct your course. Next comes grieving the loss truth brings. I needed to face the lost time involved in pursuing a project I would now drop. Discernment often brings the need to confront far more serious losses. When you realize a good friend or family member has been dishonest with you, discernment may protect you from further harm, but you will need to grieve the loss of trust within the relationship.

If discernment helps you see the error in a false teaching, you will face the loss of comfort that false teaching once brought you. If the matter is important, you may seek fellowship with a different faith community, losing a network of friendships in the process. Discernment may lead to confrontation, to endings and to unwanted change. Discernment takes courage as much as wisdom. Ignoring the doubts can feel easier. Procrastinating a decision may be more palatable than facing difficult truth. However, growth and progress require working through your doubts and making the necessary decisions. Better to face your losses now than invest years in a false belief system. Better to confront a friend than suffer loss to your reputation from gossip, to your finances through dishonesty or to your heart from betrayal.

I sat with my legs stretched out in front of me on the white sands of Sconset Beach and watched the waves break on the shoreline. My eyes followed the water to where the ocean met the sky on the horizon, taking in the vastness of the rows of crashing waves. I sensed my insignificance within this landscape and began to grasp the trivial nature of my concerns against the complexity of creation. I imagined the numerous beaches across the planet. On how many beaches were people staring at the shoreline, pondering a future decision? Long after my decision was a distant memory, these waves would roll in, slowly changing the landscape, yet timeless in their ongoing rhythm. My decision would not perturb the waves.

One of my favorite Bible verses is 2 Corinthians 4:6, "For God, who said, 'Let light shine out of darkness,' made his light to shine in our hearts to give us the light of the knowledge of God's glory displayed in the face of Christ." This verse presents the challenge of acknowledging the majesty of God as creator alongside the intimacy of God in relationship to his creation. The ocean waves display the power of creation, seemingly too distant and strong to care about the concerns of a lone person sitting on the sand. Yet, Luke 12:6-7 reminds us, "Are not five sparrows sold for two pennies? Yet not one of them is forgotten by God. Indeed, the very hairs of your head are all numbered. Don't be afraid; you are worth more than many sparrows." To receive the wisdom that God promises, we must see him as the God of the waves, powerful enough to provide, as well as the God of the sparrows, compassionate enough to care for our needs.

At some point the cloud of confusion and uncertainty gives way to peace. The Bible speaks of the peace that transcends all understanding (Phil 4:7). This peace helps you discern that you have made the right decision. Although your decision may bring you challenges and even hardships, God's peace gives you the courage to proceed. Nehemiah, a Jew who was a high official in the Persian court, correctly discerned that Sanballat and his comrades were seeking to discredit his work of restoring the walls around Jerusalem (Neh 6). This realization, a fruit of Nehemiah's prayers, protected his leadership and the work he set out to accomplish. He stood his ground and did not give in to fear, even when he received a death threat.

Such peace is a gift. It comes after you have examined the data, sought guidance from wise counselors and prayed for direction. It is the bookend to your initial doubts that started the discerning process. It is the moment when you are ready to stand up, leave the ocean behind and face a future shaped by your decision.

Of course, discernment applies to areas not addressed in Scripture. You do not need to doubt or pray about a decision that would be counter to biblical principles. For example, if your boss asks you to do something unethical, you do not need to question whether to follow his directives. However, you may need to seek guidance in how to respond to your boss and whether you should pursue new employment.

Discernment is also not an excuse to rely on feelings and hunches in place of reason and good advice. Proverbs 12:15 warns rather bluntly,

The way of fools seems right to them,
    but the wise listen to advice.

Proverbs 14:12 underscores the point:

There is a way that appears to be right,
    but in the end it leads to death.

Feeling without facts can be dangerous. Consider Saul before he became Paul the apostle. He explains in his own words,

I too was convinced that I ought to do all that was possible to oppose the name of Jesus of Nazareth. And that is just what I did in Jerusalem. On the authority of the chief priests I put many of the Lord's people in prison, and when they were put to death, I cast my vote against them. Many a time I went from one synagogue to another to have them punished, and I tried to force them to blaspheme. I was so obsessed with persecuting them that I even hunted them down in foreign cities. (Acts 26:9-11)

Saul felt that he was doing the right thing in his religious zeal. However, he was harming others and opposing his Savior. Feelings were an insufficient guide to right behavior. Saul needed an experience and a confrontation, which he found on the road to Damascus (Acts 9:3-9). Yet after the light from heaven, the voice of God and three days spent blind, he also needed the gentle, restoring words of Ananias, who treated Saul as a brother in spite of his past actions and became the vessel that brought healing to him. The combination put Saul, now Paul, on the correct path.

However, for those areas where you need direction or confirmation of an action otherwise in line with scriptural principles and based on sound reasoning, the peace that comes as you face a difficult decision can be valuable confirmation of your new direction or understanding. Along with peace, I enjoyed a tailwind on my ride back to the bed and breakfast. With my mind clear and my heart settled, I was prepared to explore the island without distraction.

MAKING A DECISION

One place I wanted to visit was the Old Mill, the country's oldest working wind-powered grain mill, built in 1746 by a seaman named Nathan Wilbur, who designed the mill after the ones he had seen in Holland. While the building was fixed, the top of the mill could be turned to face the sails into the wind in a design called a smock mill. Wilbur constructed the building's framework with beams washed ashore from shipwrecked vessels. Wood lost at sea found a new use in a powerful new mill that could grind five bushels of corn an hour.

Faith often requires us to believe that what was shipwrecked can be put to powerful use once again. When we move forward from a loss, we trust good will come from the experience. Of course, the beams washed ashore never sailed the ocean again. When you make a difficult decision, you may sustain a loss never recovered again in its original form. Hope for believers going through difficult situations they do not understand is found in Romans 8:28: "And we know that in all things God works for the good of those who love him, who have been called according to his purpose." Someday a charming and useful windmill may gather the ocean breezes on a hill overlooking the sea that once brought calamity.

After the Old Mill, I explored a whaling museum and ducked in and out of many delightful shops along the cobblestone streets. In the shops and over the shoulders of ladies walking down the street, I saw lightship baskets that function as summer purses, festooned with scrimshaw art—etching in ivory filled with ink. These baskets, steeped in Nantucket history going as far back as the early nineteenth century, once were made on lightships stationed around the island to mark dangerous shoals in areas where lighthouse construction was untenable. For example, the hazardous Nantucket Shoals south of the island were marked by the Lightship Nantucket. This lightship station, established in 1854, provided the first beacon seen by vessels approaching the United States from a transatlantic voyage.

The men stationed on these lightships for thirty-day stretches passed the time by weaving beautiful lightship baskets. A tradition formed to place a penny inside the lightship basket. In 1977, Glenaan Elliott Robbins turned the lightship basket into jewelry. She designed a miniature version of the lightship basket in gold and sold these creations in her store on Straight Wharf, known as The Golden Basket. The little lightship baskets, worn as pendants, are decorated with scrimshaw designs and have swinging handles and working hinges.

When you open the basket lid, you find a miniature copper penny hidden inside, in keeping with the tradition started for lightship baskets. Most of the lightship baskets are topped with scrimshaw designs of ships, whales, flowers or lighthouses. However, when I walked through The Golden Basket, I found a unique necklace with a lightship basket decorated with a scrimshaw design of the Old Mill.

I am not a person quick to purchase a souvenir, but I was drawn to the golden lightship basket with the Old Mill on top. For a graduate student, such a necklace would be a luxury. I wrestled with the decision to purchase the necklace and left the store to explore other sites around Nantucket. The day I was to board the ferry and leave the island, I returned and made the purchase. I have never regretted the decision.

The necklace became a reminder to me that joy can arise on the other side of a difficult decision. My concerns about choosing the right research direction seem so trivial to me now, but I remember the emotions I felt that April. Perhaps less of my future rested on that decision than I believed at the time. Balance between work goals and family goals came with time. My research direction became a source of intellectual adventure and a useful contribution to cancer research. Of course, the true test of a decision is the test of time. If I could travel back to that moment at Sconset Beach now, I would made the decision in a snap and then go fly a kite above the ocean waves with carefree abandon.

Our ability to make decisions is one of the gifts God has given us. Consider Moses standing on a mountain before the children of Israel, giving the people his last words of instruction before he goes on to Mount Nebo, where he will die.

This day I call the heavens and the earth as witnesses against you that I have set before you life and death, blessings and curses. Now choose life, so that you and your children may live and that

you may love the LORD your God, listen to his voice, and hold
fast to him. For the LORD is your life, and he will give you many
years in the land he swore to give to your fathers, Abraham, Isaac
and Jacob. (Deut 30:19-20)

We have the ability to choose life, to choose integrity, to choose the
path of future blessings for ourselves and for our families. We are not
trapped by destiny or powerless in our decisions.

However, this ability to make decisions is tempered by our humanity. As the prophet Isaiah reminds the people,

All people are like grass,
    and all their faithfulness is like the flowers of the field.
The grass withers and the flowers fall,
    because the breath of the LORD blows on them.
    Surely the people are grass.
The grass withers and the flowers fall,
    but the word of our God endures forever. (Is 40:6-8)

This passage is a reminder of the brevity of human life and God's
sovereignty. Just as the daffodils brightened Nantucket for a few weeks
in April, then faded from glory, our time on this earth is short. Acci-
dents and illnesses can cut that time even shorter and without much
notice. Our decisions stand in tension between our accountability for
our actions and our vulnerability to the larger forces of nature. We
sense our power to change the course of history while acknowledging
we can fade from its pages in an instance. A combination of the humility born from recognizing our frailty and the responsibility given by
our free will creates the proper mindset for making decisions.

At times we may discern incorrectly and make costly mistakes. In
these times, we rely on God's redemptive love to help us find our way.
The purpose of the gospel message is

> to bind up the brokenhearted,
>> to proclaim freedom for the captives
>> and release from darkness for the prisoners. (Is 61:1)

The gospel provides hope beyond mistakes as well as encouragement to turn around and make a different decision.

I bought raspberry limeade at the juice stand before boarding the ferry to return to Hyannis with my husband. The vacation was over all too soon. I moved to the stern of the boat to watch the island fade into the distance as the seagulls swirled overhead. In a little more than two hours, the ferry would dock on Cape Cod, and an hour and a half later I would be back home planning my next experiment.

The mounting doubts that plagued me on the way to Nantucket were a gift that brought new focus and fresh vision on my return trip. Without the doubts, I would have invested several more months headed in an unproductive direction. While my doubts concerned a scientific project, doubts can be helpful in everyday life situations as well. A call to a new ministry or job often starts with restlessness with the current situation and a desire to take on a new challenge. Misgivings about a coworker who undermines another coworker's contributions to the team may be a warning to set stronger boundaries in the workplace. If a pastor explores his feelings of discomfort about a particular fad teaching that lacks a strong biblical basis, he may prevent error from spreading throughout a local church. Before dismissing any uneasiness I feel about a particular situation, I consider whether the feeling has a rational basis. If I find such a basis, I pray about the matter and seek guidance from a reliable friend or mentor.

The golden lightship necklace has become one of my most worn pieces of jewelry. Its cost divided over the years of service has made it one of the most economical purchases of my life. Whenever I face a challenging decision with an uncertain but critical outcome, I take the necklace off, open up the miniature basket and shake out the tiny penny. I remember that happiness belongs to the person with the courage to make a decision and move forward.

4

SOLVING PROBLEMS
WITH QUESTIONS

To raise new questions, new possibilities,
to regard old problems from a new angle requires
a creative imagination and marks
the real advances in science.

ALBERT EINSTEIN

After three days they found him in
the temple courts, sitting among the teachers,
listening to them and asking them questions.
Everyone who heard him was amazed at his
understanding and his answers.

LUKE 2:46-47

"THE ONLY STUPID QUESTION is the one you do not ask." I overheard a postdoctoral student making this remark to a new graduate student joining our lab for a rotation. From the hesitant look on the new student's face, I could sense his reluctance to believe this axiom. However, trust in this statement is the difference between an accomplished researcher and a neophyte. This concept also differentiates the researcher in command of lab safety from the accident waiting to happen.

I believe in questions both inside and outside the laboratory. Questions sharpen our thinking and provide a way to test subjective experience. Questions are a way to connect with other people and accept their help. Questions are a protection against confusion, oversights and exploitation. Questions provide definition, clarity and focus. Problem solving, especially in the practice of science, relies on questions.

Scientists attend conferences not so much to listen to speakers as to ask probing questions of those speakers. The questions not only help scientists gather useful information, but they allow scientists to link that information to their own research interests. If questions can help scientists find new cures for diseases and send a man to the moon, then perhaps questions also have a place in the realm of faith.

LEARNING AND CONNECTING WITH QUESTIONS

One of the privileges of making progress on one's thesis research is the opportunity to attend a scientific conference at least once a year. In the Boston and Cambridge area, local scientific meetings are of high caliber because of the close proximity of so many excellent universities, hospitals and research institutes. However, fresh research insights require thinking in new ways and integrating discoveries in your field from around the world. Therefore, specialized scientific conferences that draw top researchers in a given field provide the chance to learn about exciting new research discoveries before they are published in scientific journals.

The Keystone Symposia are a great example of the open, peer-reviewed conferences that accelerate progress in the life sciences. Founded in 1972 in Los Angeles by a molecular biology professor, the organization moved to Silverthorne, Colorado, in 1990. Various conferences on important topics in molecular biology were held at the Keystone Resort in Keystone, Colorado, as well as at other ski resorts in Colorado and New Mexico. Today the conferences are held in locations in addition to ski resorts, such as the Boston Park Plaza and Towers and a hotel in Stockholm, Sweden.

One of the features that make conferences like the Keystone Symposia wonderful for graduate students is the opportunity to present your work on a poster set up in a ballroom at the resort. To qualify for this privilege, you must submit an abstract to the meeting organizers months in advance. If the abstract describing your research is approved, the abstract is published in a book given to all conference attendees, and you can set up a display describing your research during a poster session. Poster sessions are the grown-up versions of science fairs, but without any prizes other than the opportunity to network with colleagues and add a line to your curriculum vitae.

The conference speakers are well-known scientists invited by the conference organizers. Without the concept of a poster session, graduate students would be relegated to the role of spectators instead of participants. During the fifteen-minute talks by the invited speakers, you view slides of research findings projected on the wall. At the end of each talk, time is allowed for several questions from the audience. Usually other senior scientists ask these questions. While the information from the talks is very useful, the poster sessions allow you to examine the research findings as long as you desire. You can engage in a conversation with the researcher standing next to his poster, learning details about an experimental protocol or questioning the interpretation of the scientific findings. These conversations may help you realize how someone else's finding provides the perfect puzzle piece to move your own research forward. Maybe the conversation simply sparks a great idea, or perhaps two distant labs decide to collaborate.

A graduate student presenting her own poster has an opportunity to discuss her research with other interested scientists. Many times helpful ideas come from these discussions. I have found I learn more from these scientific conversations than from any other aspect of a conference.

After I arrived at the Keystone Resort and picked up the conference schedule, I realized the conference organizers were wise and practical people who had arranged the schedule to accommodate afternoon skiing. Make no mistake—scientists work long hours, even at ski resorts. The talks by the invited speakers started early in the morning and ran to lunch. They resumed after dinner and ran late into the night. However, the incomparable soft, deep powder on the Colorado ski slopes was the agenda item for early afternoon. For dedicated scientists, après-ski, the relaxing time after skiing, took the form of two poster sessions late each afternoon before dinner. Two sessions gave you the opportunity to present your own poster for one session and then walk through the exhibit hall to meet other scientific researchers and view their posters for the second session.

One evening the agenda provided time for other resort activities, and I signed up for a sleigh-ride dinner with my husband. At the front of the resort, a wrangler helped us into the two-person sleigh and adjusted the warm wool blanket that protected us from the falling snow. He hopped into the front of the sleigh, and we set off on a thirty-minute ride across Soda Creek Valley to a rustic shelter where another wrangler was already preparing our dinner. The soft music of the sleigh bells was punctuated by our wrangler sharing historical information about the area and tidbits about modern-day cowboy life.

Although the blanket kept me warm, the chilly air and wet snow made me grateful for the warmth within the shelter when we arrived. On this particular night, all the other patrons had signed up for later time slots, so we enjoyed the first serving of dinner for the day alone with two wranglers. I have never tasted a better steak before or since this dinner. Potatoes, beans and biscuits rounded out the meal, and warm, spicy cowboy cake finished the dining experience. During the meal, we enjoyed the simple entertainment of singing and guitar playing from a musically gifted cowboy.

In keeping with the spirit of the scientific conference, I enjoyed the opportunity to ask the cowboys questions and to answer their questions about the life of a scientist in Boston. By the time dinner was over and we climbed into the sleigh for our return trip through the woods and across a snowy field to the resort, the cowboys felt like old friends. Such is the power of questions to connect people.

Good questions solve problems of understanding. They bridge cultural and socioeconomic differences by helping us gather the necessary information to better understand another person's perspective. Good questions can show us what information we lack. Scientists will often ask a series of questions to step their way through a problem, with each question bringing more focus to their thinking. Wise teachers make use of questions to get their students to think. The Socratic method is based on asking and answering questions in order to hone critical thinking skills.

A careful reading of the Gospel accounts shows Jesus using questions in his ministry. He understood the gap that grows between intentions and actions and asked questions about priorities.

And why do you worry about clothes? (Mt 6:28)

Couldn't you men keep watch with me for one hour? (Mt 26:40)

Why are you sleeping? (Lk 22:46)

Questions help us confront our limitations with greater honesty than do accusations or open rebuke. Instead of becoming defensive, we must stop and consider the driving force behind our behavior. Jesus also understood that faith goes beyond intellectual assent. He knew that a good question presses beyond mere information to address the emotions driving our choices.

Why are you so afraid? (Mk 4:40)

Why are you crying? (Jn 20:15)

Does this offend you? (Jn 6:61)

Jesus also knew we were made for a greater purpose than mere survival through our daily routine. He asked people questions to help them get their focus beyond their immediate concerns to the larger spiritual truths.

But what about you? . . . Who do you say I am? (Mt 16:15)

What do you want me to do for you? (Mt 20:32)

Why are you thinking these things in your hearts? (Lk 5:22)

From these examples, we see that questions can challenge and strengthen our faith and help us solve problems in our spiritual life. Of course, questions can become stumbling blocks if used in the wrong manner. Questions should help us learn more, not become an excuse to be argumentative. Questions should illuminate our thinking, not become a defense against new ideas. Questions should connect us to people, not drive a wedge in relationships. Ultimately, questions can help us resolve our doubts instead of letting them fester.

DEFEATING FALSE ASSUMPTIONS WITH QUESTIONS

The scientific method revolves around the concept of a testable hypothesis. A working hypothesis can be stated in a variety of formats. Suppose you were planning on testing whether sunlight is essential for the development of bean seedlings. You could state your working hypothesis as a conditional statement: "Sunlight may be essential for the development of bean seedlings." You could also state the hypothesis as an if-then statement: "If sunlight is essential for the development of bean seedlings, then growing seedlings in the dark will decrease the maturation rate of the seedlings." Finally, you can phrase your hypothesis as a question: "Is sunlight essential for the development of bean seedlings?"

Even if you construct your working hypothesis as a conditional statement or an if-then statement, you are testing a question in your experiment design. Questions also become important later in the experimental process. After you analyze experimental data, questions can help you interpret the results by revealing hidden assumptions that affect how you draw conclusions.

Back in Boston, I learned a lesson about hidden assumptions the day after my car was stolen from the hospital parking lot near my research lab. My car was a gray Oldsmobile, of practical value to me but certainly not a flashy sports car that should attract thieves. I bought the car right after my college graduation, my first car purchase, so it had sentimental value as well. Upon calling the Boston police, I discovered that thieves target cars of all types to strip for parts at "chop shops." Thus, finding your car in the first twenty-four hours after it is stolen is critical. The next day I talked to the attendant in the lot where the car was stolen. I was taken aback by his attitude. "Oh, you rich doctors can just buy another car. What does it matter?"

As a third-year graduate student with many years to go until graduation, I was neither rich nor a doctor. I came to realize that the attendant assumed anyone involved in medical research must be paid well. In fact, full-time graduate students and parking lot attendants share a similar pay scale. Of course, a graduate student can look forward to increased earning potential in the future, but future earnings do not buy cars for the present.

I took a moment to explain the financial realities of graduate school to the attendant. He struggled to believe my words and let go of his false assumptions. Fortunately, the police found my car before it was dismantled, the only loss being an emergency tool kit in the trunk. My interaction with the parking lot attendant reminded me of the danger of making assumptions about people. Insufficient data can cause a scientist to draw the wrong conclusions in the laboratory, and assumptions based on partial information can create serious problems in life. The student in the back of the class who rarely participates may not be aloof or disengaged but simply shy. The elderly person in the wheelchair does not have hearing or comprehension problems and would prefer you address her instead of her attendant. The coworker sitting idly at his desk may not be daydreaming but thinking through a difficult problem.

Assumptions can cross over to become stereotypes if we make a judgment about an individual based on our thoughts about a certain group or category of people. For example, we may believe the stereotype that girls excel in writing but struggle in mathematics. As a result, Melinda, a girl with a strong aptitude for math, may not receive the same encouragement to pursue a career in the sciences as Justin, an equally talented boy in her class. Assumptions about certain categories of people can degrade into racism and prejudice.

Unfortunately, history reveals instances of scientists attempting to use experimental data to support racist notions. A well-known example is the use of craniometry, measurement of interior skull volume, to infer the intellectual superiority of certain racial and ethnic groups. In the nineteenth century, the British used this pseudoscience to justify their discriminatory policies toward Irish and black Africans by arguing that the skulls of people in these groups resembled the shape of Cro-Magnon men with similarities to apes.

In France, Paul Broca (1824–1880) concluded that women are less intelligent than men after weighing brains taken from autopsies in four Paris hospitals. He collected 292 brains of men and 140 brains of women and measured the average weight of the male brains (1325 grams) and the female brains (1144 grams), finding a difference of 181 grams between the two averages. His assumption was that brain size is an indicator of intelligence. As a result, he believed that higher education would not be good for women since their brains could not handle the work involved.[1]

Alfred Binet (1857–1911) started out as a proponent of craniometry, until his experimental results caused him to doubt the method. He measured the head size of young school children and found the differences between the higher-functioning and lower-functioning students to be negligible. Thus, he looked for more scientifically sound methods of measuring intelligence and developed an intelligence test based on skills of increasing difficulty. This test became the first practical Intelligence Quotient (IQ) test, and the forerunner of the Stanford-Binet Intelligence Scales still in use today. The false assumption of all the scientists in the field of craniometry was that cranium size and shape corresponded to intelligence. When a false assumption is shared by a group of people, challenging that assumption can be difficult. Craniometry findings supported the societal biases prevalent at the time, so scientists were inclined to believe that the assumption behind their results was accurate. Only the repeated, careful experiments of a researcher of Alfred Binet's caliber challenged the paradigm.

Assumptions in church life can hinder fellowship and cause unneeded conflict. In large, growing churches where people do not know each other well, categorizing people by assumptions can become a shortcut that substitutes for developing authentic relationships with one another. For example, members may perceive a person who does not participate in many events as uninterested in church life. If someone reached out to the person and asked the right question, the truth might surface that the person had to take a second job to make ends meet in tough economic times.

On the other hand, a well-dressed family sitting together in the pew every week may be hiding secret sorrow. Only God knows the hearts and makes no false assumptions. Even a prophet can judge a person by the wrong standards. When the prophet Samuel came to Bethlehem to anoint one of Jesse's sons as the new king to follow Saul, Israel's first king, Samuel was ready to make the wrong selection. Samuel saw Eliab, Jesse's firstborn son, and thought he had found the one who should be the next king. However, the Lord said to Samuel, "Do not consider his appearance or his height, for I have rejected him. The LORD does not look at the things people look at. People look at the outward appearance, but the LORD looks at the heart" (1 Sam 16:7).

Samuel then had seven of Jesse's eight sons pass in front of him. The Lord had not chosen any of them, although Samuel did not understand why any one of them should not be king. Samuel then asked Jesse if he had any more sons. The youngest son was tending the sheep, and Samuel sent for him. This son was the one to become King David, the next king of Israel.

In the New Testament, James warns against assumptions that produce favoritism.

> Suppose a man comes into your meeting wearing a gold ring and fine clothes, and a poor man in filthy old clothes also comes in. If you show special attention to the man wearing fine clothes and say, "Here's a good seat for you," but say to the poor man, "You stand there" or "Sit on the floor by my feet," have you not discriminated among yourselves and become judges with evil thoughts? (Jas 2:2-4)

A common assumption in some church circles affected by prosperity thinking is that wealth correlates with spirituality. However, a poor man may be closer to God than the rich man who appears outwardly blessed. Consider individuals who pursue less lucrative careers in order to make a difference in people's lives. Their incomes may not allow them to purchase the high-end suits that corporate executives can purchase, but their value in the kingdom of God is no less. Difficult events in life may cause people in the church to struggle in their careers, in their family life or with their health. However, we must be careful not to make assumptions about their spiritual life or their importance to the church.

Of course, we would be incorrect to make false assumptions about the wealthy within our churches as well. Their jobs may limit their church participation, especially if they must travel frequently. However, wealthy individuals often give freely from their resources to support the church, playing an important role in the life of the church community. While they may have more material possessions than others, they may also shoulder more leadership responsibilities in their careers.

False assumptions can create misunderstandings in church ministries. Perhaps the young couple with no children does not feel called to work in the children's ministries of the church. Perhaps a woman with a career in finance would rather serve on a church committee that used her professional skills than in the more traditional women's ministry. Perhaps an older woman whose children are grown enjoys caring for babies in the nursery. Simply asking people about their passions and interests can prevent misplaced and disheartened volunteers.

In our efforts to be helpful and minister to people, we must be willing to show them respect by asking questions instead of jumping to conclusions. Be careful not to project your needs onto someone else. Some young mothers feel depressed after childbirth, but many do not. A man may not talk openly about his grief after the death of a loved one, although he may process his grief by taking actions. Trying to force a person into a certain ministry mold may not help the person although our intentions may be admirable. Questions allow us to tailor our response to the needs of the individual.

False assumptions about religion and science can create barriers to faith. Consider the statement by particle physicist, philosopher, author and religious skeptic Victor J. Stenger, "Science flies us to the moon. Religion flies us into buildings."[2] The two sentences are based on historical facts. On July 20, 1969, the *Eagle* landed on the moon, and astronauts Neil Armstrong and Buzz Aldrin left bootprints in the lunar soil. On September 11, 2001, nineteen al-Qaeda terrorists hijacked four airplanes, successfully flying two planes into the Twin Towers of the World Trade Center complex in New York City and a third plane into the Pentagon in Washington, D.C. Radical Muslim religious beliefs accounted for part of the motivation for the deadly attacks. However, the overall statement holds the hidden assumption that science produces only good outcomes while religious beliefs produce only violence and destruction.

History shows that neither science nor religion can claim exclusively good or bad effects on society. The field of bioethics developed in the twentieth century in response to the experiments Nazi doctors conducted on death camp prisoners in Europe and scandals in the United States involving human experimentation, such as doctors deliberately infecting mentally retarded children with the hepatitis virus at the Willowbrook State School in New York in the early 1960s or denying medical treatment to 399 poor, African American men in the Tuskegee Syphilis Study from 1932 to 1972.[3] Patients in these studies were harmed in the name of science, not religion. Humanitarian efforts by Christian organizations such as Compassion International, World Vision and Convoy of Hope have fed the hungry, educated children and delivered emergency supplies to regions devastated by hurricanes, typhoons, earthquakes, tornadoes and wildfires. You could look at these examples and say, "In the face of human suffering, religion offers compassion while science responds with indifference." Such a statement would be accurate for the examples I offered, but no more fair than the statement made by Stenger. The question that defeats the false assumptions for both my statement and Stenger's is, are there other examples that could disprove the validity of this statement? After I recovered my car, I realized I had made a false assumption about the safety of my car in the attended hospital parking lot. I bought an antitheft steering-wheel lock for my car to prevent any future problems. When the gray paint on my car wore thin, I had the car repainted a bright red. The bright red version of my car served me well for another decade and, in spite of the flashier color, was never stolen. The lesson the parking lot attendant taught me about hidden assumptions still serves me to this day.

MAINTAINING FOCUS WITH QUESTIONS

While graduate school means a lengthy stretch of financial sacrifice in the name of education and future opportunities, it also provides the gift of a clear focus. The path for five or more years of your life is well defined. First comes coursework, then qualifying exams, then a thesis proposal, then years of thesis research, followed by the thesis defense. The objective is to complete your doctoral degree and contribute new knowledge to your scientific field.

During graduate school, your tasks for the next several years are set in stone. You do not need to look around for new hobbies or activities to fill your calendar. Conducting experiments and writing scientific papers will fill your days and nights for the foreseeable future. Your objective narrows your choices, and you achieve focus on a singular goal.

Many times problem solving is a process of clarification. From the smorgasbord of choices, we narrow the possibilities. Like a detective in a mystery novel, we use each clue to help us rule out possible suspects. In life, commitments narrow choices. When a high school senior chooses a college, he decides against attending all the other schools in the country. When a student declares a major, she is choosing what she will not study as well as the subject that will get her greatest attention. In a wedding ceremony, two individuals decide to forsake all others and be faithful to one another. This concept comes from Genesis 2:24, "That is why a man leaves his father and mother and is united to his wife, and they become one flesh."

For our faith to be successful, we need to make a commitment and choose a focus. Hebrews 12:1-2 provides instructions: "Let us run with perseverance . . . fixing our eyes on Jesus, the pioneer and perfecter of faith. For the joy set before him he endured the cross, scorning its shame, and sat down at the right hand of the throne of God." Jesus had a singular goal. He came "to seek and to save the lost" (Lk 19:10). He kept in mind the great joy of finding the lost and reconciling them to himself. He described this joy to his disciples through parables. He told the story of the shepherd with one hundred sheep who lost one of them. Upon discovering one sheep was missing, he left the other ninety-nine in the open country to search for the one lost sheep. When he found his lost sheep, he put it on his shoulders, returned home and threw a big party for all his friends and neighbors to celebrate (Lk 15:3-7).

Anticipation of this joy helped Jesus handle excruciating pain when the Roman soldiers drove spikes through his hands and feet to nail him to the cross. He persevered past the shame of a humiliating public execution and took his rightful place as the Son of God and Savior of humankind. He achieved his singular goal of paying the high price of redemption so he could rescue the lost and reunite them with their heavenly Father. The Christian faith revolves around the meaning of Jesus' death and subsequent resurrection. His sacrifice and his example must be the focus of every Christian believer.

When doubts creep in to the lives of Christians through events or experiences, they often begin to lose focus. Perhaps a close friend dies by suicide or perishes in a car accident. Maybe illness, divorce or a financial reversal turns a family's life upside down overnight. Suddenly, faith becomes complicated. How could this happen if God really loves me? Why were my prayers not answered? Does God even exist?

The way to spiritual health through such storms of life starts with blocking out the distractions and concentrating on what matters most. "Set your minds on things above, not on earthly things" (Col 3:2). Earthly difficulties, while real, must not divert our attention from eternal things. We do not need to deny the reality of the pain we feel over losses or hardships. The apostle Paul talked about his difficulties in his second letter to the Corinthian believers.

> For when we came into Macedonia, we had no rest, but we were harassed at every turn—conflicts on the outside, fears within. But God, who comforts the downcast, comforted us by the coming of Titus, and not only by his coming but also by the comfort you had given him. He told us about your longing for me, your deep sorrow, your ardent concern for me, so that my joy was greater than ever. (2 Cor 7:5-7)

Paul experienced unrelenting difficulties from all directions. He experienced beatings, imprisonments and riots. He worked hard through hunger and sleepless nights. He was a genuine minister of the gospel, but those he longed to reach sometimes regarded him as an imposter. Many believers knew him, yet those who should have honored him treated him as unknown. He had nothing by earthly standards but everything by heavenly standards (2 Cor 6:5-10).

Paul lived in constant danger because of his ministry. In his words, "I have been in danger from rivers, in danger from bandits, in danger from my fellow Jews, in danger from Gentiles; in danger in the city, in danger in the country, in danger at sea; and in danger from false believers" (2 Cor 11:26). In the midst of physical hardships, those people within the church world that he trusted caused him grief. He had conflicts on the outside. The pressure from all the external stress caused fears within. We can imagine the fears for safety, for reputation and for the welfare of the churches.

Paul knew the importance of focusing on what mattered. As he explained in his first letter to the Corinthians,

> Jews demand signs and Greeks look for wisdom, but we preach Christ crucified: a stumbling block to Jews and foolishness to Gentiles, but to those whom God has called, both Jews and Greeks, Christ the power of God and the wisdom of God. For the foolishness of God is wiser than human wisdom, and the weakness of God is stronger than human strength. (1 Cor 1:22-25)

Paul focused on the message of the cross and God's desire to reconcile humanity to himself. He knew this message of redemption was more important than displays of God's miraculous power or nuggets of theological wisdom.

In the midst of holding on to what he knew was true, Paul found comfort. God provided Paul with a friend in Titus, who came with messages of care and concern from the church in Corinth. Titus brought reconciliation between Paul and the church in Corinth and addressed the problems in the church that had caused Paul grief. In the midst of Paul's weakness, God showed himself strong. Through Titus, God solved the problem that Paul could not solve on his own.

Perhaps these experiences led Paul to write, "We are hard pressed on every side, but not crushed; perplexed, but not in despair; persecuted, but not abandoned; struck down, but not destroyed" (2 Cor 4:8-9). The constant pressures, conflicts and challenges taught Paul that although troubles come, God delivers. The difficulties did not crush Paul's ministry. The questions in his heart that left him perplexed stopped short of despair. Although both nonbelievers and false teachers persecuted him, God did not abandon him. He was beaten, stoned, shipwrecked, flogged and thrown into prison (2 Cor 11:23-25), but not destroyed. He lived out the proverb,

> Let your eyes look straight ahead;
> fix your gaze directly before you. (Prov 4:25)

Paul had a singular goal: to preach the gospel.

The doubts that help you solve problems will move you in a positive direction toward the solution. Doubts that tear down your confidence or destroy your faith take you down the path to confusion. Asking questions of your doubts permits you to differentiate between the two. Paul did not push away his fears. He endured past them. He developed a faith strong enough to handle human weakness (2 Cor 12:9-10). God did not remove his thorn in the flesh, end the persecution or silence his critics. However, God showed Paul a faith beyond his doubts.

When you are attempting to discern whether a particular goal is worth pursuing, consider asking yourself the following questions: Will I have the greatest impact if I pursue this goal instead of other competing goals? Is this goal a good fit with my abilities? Does this goal line up with my passions? Will the return on investment justify the cost of pursuing this goal? Will I have access to the necessary resources to finish what I start? Is this goal consistent with my calling and values? Once you have made a commitment to pursue a given goal, recognize that problems will arise. Sometimes you may need to make course corrections, but abandoning a well-thought-out, carefully discerned goal should be a rare event in your life.

Judah Folkman, a professor at Harvard Medical School who conducted research at Children's Hospital in Boston when I was a graduate student, spent more than twenty years testing the hypothesis that tumors might be able to stimulate the development of new blood vessels to feed their own growth, a process he labeled angiogenesis. He felt that inhibiting this process could be the key to fighting cancer. For many years, other cancer researchers failed to recognize the value of his idea. His persistence changed the course of medicine, with angiogenesis-inhibiting drugs being used to treat millions of patients with cancer and other diseases that involve the production of new blood vessels, such as macular degeneration.[4]

When asked how he remained dedicated to his ideas over the course of four decades, even when facing sustained skepticism from many in the scientific community, he replied, "I have come to realize that the key is to choose a problem that is worth persistent effort." He taught his students to ask "burning questions," which he defined as scientific questions that would have a major impact in the lives of patients. In his lab, he filled a whiteboard with questions crucial to patients, questions that others might write off as either irrelevant or too big to tackle. When a lab member accepted the challenge to seek an answer to one of the questions, he would write that person's initials next to the question, where they would remain until the question was answered.[5]

Graduate school taught me that following a singular goal could take you to the top of a Colorado ski mountain or to the stolen-car recovery lot in the heart of the city of Boston. Every journey has high moments and low moments, and the journey of faith is no different. Even at twelve years of age, Jesus knew the value of asking questions in order to learn and to teach (Lk 2:46-47). Albert Einstein, the famous theoretical physicist, understood that the best way to gain insight into intractable problems is to ask a fresh question. Doubts can be a gift capable of leading you to the truth you were missing. They can function like the mirror in a car, helping a driver to see an approaching car entering his blind spot. Sometimes a certain make of car retains a blind spot invisible to the driver even with the help of mirrors. In the same way, we will stumble upon situations where the best a question can do is reveal our limits. Not every question has an answer. But a question is often a good place to start in attempting to solve a problem.

Part Two

Sources of Doubt

5

LOCATING LIMITS

With increasing distance, our knowledge fades,
and fades rapidly. Eventually, we reach the dim boundary—
the utmost limits of our telescopes. There, we measure shadows,
and we search among ghostly errors of measurement for landmarks
that are scarcely more substantial. The search will continue.
Not until the empirical resources are exhausted, need we
pass onto the dreamy realms of speculation.

EDWIN POWELL HUBBLE

Now we see only a reflection as in a mirror;
then we shall see face to face. Now I know in part;
then I shall know fully, even as I am fully known.

1 CORINTHIANS 13:12

THE STRONG BREEZE BLEW ACROSS the overlook deck on
Grandview Avenue, making a muggy August evening in Pittsburgh
more tolerable. I looked down at the treetops on the slope of Mount
Washington, then straight ahead to the skyscrapers across the river.

To the left was the famous fountain at Point State Park, and to the right, the Cathedral of Learning in Oakland. Off in the distance I saw the rolling hills of the eastern suburbs of Pittsburgh with some farmland blurring against the horizon.

I could see the veins in the leaves in the treetops just beneath the overlook and the color of the cars parked at Three Rivers Stadium, but I could not tell if any tractors plowed the farmland on the rolling hills far to the east. The level of detail faded with distance. At the limits of my visual acuity, I could see only blobs of color. At this point in the distance, the exact identity of an object became a matter of speculation.

The horizons of our knowledge work like the view from the top of Mount Washington in Pittsburgh. We have a rich array of information stretched out before us. Given the sophistication of our scientific tools, much of that information is available to an astonishing level of detail and to a vast extent. However, even the best tools of modern science blur on a distant horizon. Several of the key scientific discoveries of the twentieth century call us to embrace the uncertainty built into our universe—an uncertainty permanently beyond the reach of scientific tools.

Using the analogy of seeing an image in the mirror, the apostle Paul reminded the Christians who lived in Corinth that theology has limits as well (1 Cor 13:12). When I look in a glass mirror today, I see a fairly accurate reflection. However, the mirrors available to Paul in the first century were made of slightly convex metal polished to a high shine. These mirrors could only deliver partial knowledge within the reflection. Full knowledge of a person's image could only happen when you were looking at him face to face. Human limitations will preclude full knowledge of God and his ways during the earthly lifetimes of believers.

PUSHING THE LIMITS

The view of Pittsburgh from Mount Washington is a spectacular urban vista and high on the must-see list for tourists in the city. For me, Mount Washington is a slice of family history as well as a place with a beautiful view and upscale restaurants. My paternal grandfather moved his family of seven children to a house on Grandview Avenue long before the real estate prices for such properties soared into the millions. The Monongahela Incline was not a sightseeing stop for my grandfather but a vital component of his daily commute from the top of Mount Washington to the railroad below where he worked as a plumber on the steam locomotives.

The Monongahela Incline, built in 1870, is a cable-powered incline with two cars that operate as a pair. Each car is attached to the opposite end of a single cable, and the two cars counterbalance each other. One car goes up the incline at the same time that the other goes down. An operator at the top of the incline operates the engine that moves the cars. Because the two cars counterbalance, the role of the engine is to overcome friction and the difference between the weight of the passengers in the two cars. With a grade of 35°, 35 min, the Monongahela Incline is both the oldest and the steepest incline in Pittsburgh. The car wheels ride on rails similar to trains, with the cable in the center and wooden ties forming the inclined tracks. In theory, you could slide open the door of the car, get out and walk up the steep tracks to the station.

I have a great respect for heights, and I could not imagine myself walking up those incline tracks, but one evening when the incline cars stalled because of a cable malfunction, my grandfather did just that. He knew his family of seven children was waiting at home at the top of the mountain, and he could not wait for the operator to make the repair. He pushed himself to his limits to do what he needed to do for his family. Of course, I do not recommend climbing out of an incline car and walking up the tracks. However, circumstances often summon bravery within us that we have not recognized previously.

The challenge in life is knowing when to push the limits and when to respect the limits. Limits test our faith. Moses experienced a limit when he learned he could not enter the Promised Land (Num 20:12). Paul had to accept the limitation of the thorn in the flesh (2 Cor 12:6-9). These limitations were final. No amount of praying would change these outcomes, although prayer could bring grace and acceptance. As he prepared to see the Promised Land from the top of Mount Nebo before dying, Moses spoke these words to the children of Israel:

> I will proclaim the name of the LORD.
>   Oh, praise the greatness of our God!
> He is the Rock, his works are perfect,
>   and all his ways are just.
> A faithful God who does no wrong,
>   upright and just is he. (Deut 32:3-4)

Moses accepted God as just in his decision to keep Moses from entering the Promised Land because of his disobedience at the waters of Meribah (Num 20:2-13). Moses' faith did not remove the limitation. Instead, his faith grew strong enough to accept the limitation. In the same way, after Paul pleaded with the Lord three times to take away his thorn in the flesh, he came to accept God's grace as sufficient for his needs (2 Cor 12:6-9).

However, sometimes faith calls us to surmount presumed limits. In the Babylonian courts far from his homeland, a man named Daniel withstood treachery from other government leaders and physical danger in a lions' den to stay true to his faith (Dan 6:1-28). King Darius appointed 120 satraps, or governors, to rule throughout the Medo-Persian Empire, and three administrators in charge of them, one of whom was Daniel. The job of the administrators was to protect King Darius's interests. Daniel did such a good job that King Darius planned to set him over the whole kingdom. When they heard this news, the other administrators and the satraps sought to discredit Daniel. Backlash after success is almost a given.

Discrediting Daniel was not an easy task. The satraps could find no fault in Daniel's government dealings. Then they remembered Daniel's faith. They knew Daniel would not compromise any aspect of the law of his God or the practice of his faith. So they went to the king and appealed to his pride. They convinced the king to make a law that anyone who prays to any god or man, except to the king, during the next thirty days would be thrown into the lions' den.

Daniel saw this new law as a limit to ignore. "Three times a day he got down on his knees and prayed, giving thanks to his God, just as he had done before" (Dan 6:10). Daniel knew the consequences for disobeying the law, but he answered to a higher law. Daniel's faith knew no limits. When King Darius learned that Daniel was the victim of the new law, inspired by the satraps' appeal to the king's foolish pride, he was greatly distressed. He said to Daniel, "May your God, whom you serve continually, rescue you" (Dan 6:16). The way the law of the Medes and Persians worked was to the benefit of the satraps; once the king set a decree in motion, it could not be changed, even if the king himself regretted making the decree.

God vindicated Daniel by protecting him from the lions. However, when those who had falsely accused Daniel were thrown into the lion's den in Daniel's place, the lions crushed them almost immediately. The grateful and relieved King Darius issued a new decree stating,

> In every part of my kingdom people must fear and reverence
>   the God of Daniel.
> For he is the living God
>   and he endures forever;
> his kingdom will not be destroyed,
>   his dominion will never end. (Dan 6:26)

Daniel changed the faith of a king and a kingdom because he knew when to push past the limits set by man but not by God.

Many times we need to learn patience and stay seated in the stalled incline cars of life. However, some moments call for courage and initiative, and we must leave our comfort zone and climb the mountain. In those moments, we need to depend on the words of the apostle Paul, "If God is for us, who can be against us?" (Rom 8:31).

Good questions can help us discern the difference between times when we need to accept limits and times when we need to push the limits. For example, we might ask ourselves, Will the situation improve if I wait patiently, or will things get worse if I do not act? What is the risk of waiting versus the risk of acting? United Airlines Flight 93 was the only one of the four hijacked airplanes on September 11, 2001, that did not hit a building. The reason for the different outcome was the courage shown by the thirty-three passengers and seven crew members on this flight and the information they possessed that the passengers on the other three flights did not.

In most cases, passengers on a hijacked airplane will experience the least personal risk if they comply with the demands of the hijackers. However, the men who hijacked the airplanes on September 11, 2001, were on a suicide mission, planning to use the airplanes as missiles to destroy the lives of thousands of civilians on the ground. The hijacker who took over as pilot of Flight 93 told the passengers that a bomb was on board and the plane was returning to the airport, commanding the passengers to remain quiet and seated. However, as the passengers made phone calls to their loved ones using GTE airphones and mobile phones, they learned the fate of the three other hijacked planes. Two of the planes crashed into the Twin Towers of the World Trade Center in New York City, and the other one crashed into the Pentagon in Washington, D.C. This information changed everything.

The passengers collectively discerned that the situation called for action and courage, and they acted heroically. While their actions did not save their own lives, when Flight 93 crashed into a field in

Stonycreek Township, Pennsylvania, no one on the ground was injured. Sometimes when we decide to push the limits we make the choice for the benefit of others. When deciding whether to take the risk of action, consider how your decision will impact others and whether if both action and inaction will carry the same risk for you. You may not need to risk your life like the passengers on Flight 93 did, but you may need to step out of your comfort zone in order to make a greater impact on the world around you.

OVERLAPPING BOUNDARIES OF KNOWLEDGE

For most of my weekend escapes during my summers in graduate school, I headed south to Cape Cod and the islands of Martha's Vineyard and Nantucket. However, on rare occasions, I would drive to the shorelines north of Boston. Gloucester, a charming fishing village on Cape Ann about an hour's drive north of my research lab, became a favorite destination. The Man at the Wheel statue commemorating fishermen braving the elements on the sea symbolizes the relationship of this city to the ocean.

Sir Arthur Eddington (1882–1944), an English theoretical physicist who was one of the first scientists to appreciate the importance of Einstein's theories of special and general relativity, once gave an illustration reflecting on the limits of science. This illustration reminds me of the fisherman in Gloucester. To paraphrase Eddington, imagine an ichthyologist, or scientist who studies fish, setting out on a fishing boat early one morning to explore life in the ocean. He leaves the harbor, glances back once at the Man at the Wheel and heads for Jeffries Ledge. Once he arrives, he lets down a net with a two-inch mesh. After a while, he pulls up the net containing an assortment of sea creatures.

He surveys his catch and attempts to systematize his findings in the manner of a true scientist. After conducting his analysis, he makes two generalizations: (1) No sea creature is less than two inches long.

(2) All sea creatures have gills. Both of these generalizations are true for his catch. He hypothesizes that these generalizations will remain true if he goes fishing tomorrow as well.

The fish caught in the net of the ichthyologist represent scientific knowledge, and the net represents our senses, scientific tools and analytic skills, which we use to obtain that knowledge. A tourist walking along the harbor watching the scientist at work might point out the problem with the first generalization. "Lots of sea creatures are under two inches long. Your net is incapable of catching them." The ichthyologist rejects this objection as nonsense. "If my net can't catch them, they aren't fish." In other words, whatever knowledge cannot be measured by scientific methods is not valid and does not exist.

Of course, the scientific method is a wonderful technique for obtaining knowledge about our physical world. Thanks to science, we have been able to study both virus particles one thousand to ten thousand times smaller than the width of a human hair and the Milky Way galaxy one hundred thousand light years wide. Advances in medicine have extended the human lifespan, improved sanitation and prevented childhood diseases through vaccination. Using the knowledge of engineering, we have built bridges to span the rivers, telecommunication networks to connect people across the globe and rockets to travel to the moon.

Sir Arthur Eddington suggests we should appreciate the limits of the powerful net of science. Perhaps the question of the existence of a human soul slips through the neuroscience net. Maybe a monitor will never detect the possibility of life after death. Life may have meaning beyond the measurements we make. Like the butterfly effect that teaches we cannot predict the weather a week from now with confidence or the Heisenberg uncertainty principle that says we cannot know both the position and the speed of a particle, science may not be able to conquer all aspects of knowledge.

Science and theology come into conflict when either field oversteps its bounds. Science excels at describing aspects of the physical universe and predicting future occurrences based on past experience. Science also succeeds at dispelling false superstitions. Near the limits of scientific inquiry, the scientific method discredits myths and faulty thinking. Some scientists might venture further and say science precludes religious belief, but perhaps they have ventured too far toward the dim boundaries when knowledge gives way to speculation.

Christian theologians believe God speaks through creation (general revelation) and through his spoken and written Word (special revelation). Thus, there should be no conflict between what God has created and what he has spoken. Science studies creation, and theology studies God's Word. Both academic disciplines are fallible human attempts to understand and explain God's general and special revelation. When science and theology come into conflict, the cause is the limitation of either or both disciplines and not a problem with God.

Science does have a role in sharpening theology, even if science oversteps its bounds when it tries to discredit it. For example, the Bible contains various poetic phrases about the sun and the earth. Scholars once used some of these phrases to argue that the earth was flat.

> The LORD wraps himself in light as with a garment;
>> he stretches out the heavens like a tent
>> and lays the beams of his upper chambers on their waters.
>> (Ps 104:2-3)

This verse seems to draw a picture of a flat earth with the sky as a canopy overhead.

Another verse, Isaiah 11:12, uses the language "from the four quarters of the earth," suggesting a flat surface. However, other verses fit better with our modern understanding of the universe. For example, Job 26:7:

He spreads out the northern skies over empty space;
   he suspends the earth over nothing.

An additional verse that contradicts the idea of a flat earth is Isaiah
40:22:

He sits enthroned above the circle of the earth,
   and its people are like grasshoppers.

Of course, some scholars might argue that all these verses simply
paint poetic pictures, with some passages supporting a flat earth and
others describing modern cosmology. This ambiguity helps us locate
a limit for theology in describing the mechanisms of the physical
universe. Scientific findings can influence theological debate in a
positive way. Our modern understanding of the earth as a sphere or-
biting the sun in space helps us see confirmation in the Bible in one
set of verses and poetry in the verses that present the opposing view-
point. In this area, science sharpens theology without weakening it.

The limits of both science and theology reinforce our need for faith.
To know God, we must exercise faith in addition to intellectual effort.
Although faith operates beyond the scientific method, flowing through
the mesh of human efforts as a divine gift, faith and reason can and
should strengthen each other. Without the balance of reason, a person
can claim faith for any belief, including those with no basis in truth.
Reason alone cannot solve the great mysteries of human life, missing
certain facets of knowledge and yielding incomplete truth. Dialogue
between science and theology departments, with each field respecting
its own limits and the limits of the other, can produce a more complete
understanding of our purpose on this planet and yield a more balanced view of human experience.

In the process of training, both seminarians and scientists narrow
their academic focus in order to achieve a deep knowledge of their

specialty. Scientists experiment. Seminarians exposit. Years of pursuing different focuses create separate perspectives, which can impede dialogue between the two disciplines. The lack of dialogue can cause the two fields to dismiss each other's scholarship and miss out on the opportunity to allow one field to clarify the thinking of the other field.

Limits often occur where two academic disciplines overlap. The boundaries between two approaches to determining truth usually are soft in practice, with the power of one approach fading as the other approach strengthens. The key to understanding at these boundaries is to appreciate the contribution of the discipline whose powers of explanation are approaching its limit even while yielding to the stronger discipline. The other key to dialogue between scholars in disparate fields is to recognize the areas where one discipline possesses the preferred tools for answering a given question. Some of the most fruitful academic inquiry takes place through interdisciplinary and multidisciplinary study, as researchers use tools and resources from one discipline to shed new light on a problem within another discipline.

Biblical scholarship can inform archaeology. In fact, missionaries served as early pioneers in the disciplines of archaeology, linguistics and semiotics, hosting academic researchers on the foreign mission fields and making valuable contributions with the knowledge and insights that were a byproduct of their ministry.[1] Astronomy can inform our understanding of biblical passages containing poetic language. Medicine can formulate cures for diseases in distant lands, while ministers committed to Bible translation can become experts in preserving indigenous languages and studying intercultural dynamics. Physics can describe the properties of light in our universe while theology can illuminate our moral understanding and give life meaning. We need all academic disciplines because we miss too many fish when we only use one type of net.

EMBRACING HUMAN LIMITATIONS

In graduate school, I pushed my own limits by taking on the responsibility of leading a small youth group with my husband. Teaching teenagers is an adventure because they ask great questions and expect you to live what you believe. They also have the future stretched out before them, making them see fewer limits in life. As a result, teenagers are willing to take the risks necessary to change the world around them and shape their future. Of course, feelings of invincibility can lead to reckless behavior—a concern of every parent who hands over the car keys to a teenage son or daughter.

Although my youth group was relatively small, the questions the students asked inspired me to memorize the response, "I do not know. I will find out and get back to you." They asked the hard questions of the faith, and they deserved more than simplistic answers. I could search through a book and find answers to many of their questions, but for others, they would need to experience more of life to fully understand.

Cause and effect in life need time to play out. The time spent in training to participate in a sport, play a musical instrument or gain competence in a profession can feel like time lost to more enjoyable pursuits. A relationship or career choice that seems right at the moment may turn out to be a mistake in the next decade of life. For this reason, those who are middle-aged may regard experiences they perceived to be closed doors in their teenage years as positive events for life as a whole. The choice of a college major may become a turning point in a person's life or become irrelevant in twenty years.

Choices made later in life may have consequences that play out beyond the limits of a person's natural lifespan. Thus, the answers to the questions you ask could belong to the next generation. You may plant the apple tree but never live to taste the apples. To conclude that your apple sapling is worthless and incapable of producing fruit would be false. In the same way, a hasty judgment about the value of a decision you made or a direction in life you took may lead to a false conclusion. Questioning why God allowed a certain event in your life follows the same line of reasoning. Your pain may be real in this moment, but time may reveal a greater purpose.

Time often reveals the limitations of your abilities as well. As a teenager, almost anything seems possible. The chance to compete in the Olympics, run for president or become a billionaire is still on the table. Past the teenage years, you make decisions that narrow your choices. You may choose a mate, buy a house and embark on a certain career direction. Your dreams of the future become your present reality. You will have a certain number of children, live in certain places and grow a certain circle of friends. In choosing certain directions, you forgo other directions and embrace your limitations. Our limitations guide us in particular vocational directions, leading us toward our potential strengths. As a society, we benefit from the diversity of strengths and limitations possessed by individuals. We need doctors, theologians, farmers and merchants as well as Olympic athletes and presidents.

In addition to directing our vocational paths, our limits govern how we should relate to one another. Jesus taught his disciples to remember their own limitations before attempting to judge another person. In Luke 6:41-42, Jesus shares these words:

> Why do you look at the speck of sawdust in your brother's eye and pay no attention to the plank in your own eye? How can you say to your brother, "Brother, let me take the speck out of your eye," when you yourself fail to see the plank in your own eye? You hypocrite, first take the plank out of your eye, and then you will see clearly to remove the speck from your brother's eye.

Teenagers tend to see right and wrong as clearly black and white, wanting everyone to live up to the standards they embrace. An older person respects the standards but brings a dose of grace and humility to a situation. Older people have faced their humanity and met their limits many times. They understand the admonition found in James 3:1 and the truth in James 3:2: "Not many of you should become teachers, my fellow believers, because you know that we who teach will be judged more strictly. We all stumble in many ways. Anyone who is never at fault in what they say is perfect, able to keep their whole body in check."

Sometimes life experience makes us see limits where they do not exist. We let past failures keep us from taking new risks. Interacting with teenagers helps one look at the world through fresh eyes. Many scientific breakthroughs are developed by people relatively new to the field. They do not know where the supposed limits in a field exist so they have no problem powering beyond them. For this reason, Paul instructed Timothy, the young man he was mentoring in the faith, "Don't let anyone look down on you because you are young, but set an example for the believers in speech, in conduct, in love, in faith and in purity" (1 Tim 4:12). Young people can challenge the older generation to pursue solutions to problems thought intractable and to reach for higher standards.

My youth group challenged me to think through my beliefs so I could "be prepared to give an answer to everyone who asks you to give the reason for the hope that you have" (1 Pet 3:15). Because I became a Christian early in life and my faith grew up along with me, I did not experience as much conflict between my beliefs and my scientific pursuits. I integrated both faith and science along the journey. Several students in my youth group struggled with intellectual doubts I personally never experienced. In order to answer their questions, I had to dig deeper into the reasons behind my own beliefs. The experience enriched my own faith and challenged me to grow in new areas.

Unlike the college students I taught, who were invested in paying attention to the course material, students in my youth group had very short attention spans and no tolerance for anything "boring." If my lesson did not grab their attention in the first few minutes, I would lose them for the night. Some of the students clearly did not want to attend. They were there only because their parents were enjoying the adult service in the upstairs sanctuary. I needed to engage them quickly to move them beyond their own self-imposed limits.

Like reluctant students, believers can become impatient with God in their spiritual journey. Understanding the difficulty believers face when they need to wait, Peter reminded the early Christians,

> But do not forget this one thing, dear friends: With the Lord a day is like a thousand years, and a thousand years are like a day. The Lord is not slow in keeping his promise, as some understand slowness. Instead he is patient with you, not wanting anyone to perish, but everyone to come to repentance. (2 Pet 3:8-9)

While the concept contradicts our feelings, sometimes the limitations we experience flow from God's mercy and compassion. We wait for answers in life because God is patiently bringing us to a place where we will draw closer to him in faith. He is not denying our request but preparing a greater gift for us. Like the restless students in my class, we must learn to give our teacher the benefit of the doubt and sit still for the lesson. We will miss the life-changing truths if we tune out before the teacher shares the most important parts. In the same way unengaged students disrupt the learning experience for the entire class, believers who resist learning can cause problems for the rest of the body. When we are willing to be patient and be still, we will experience God as our fortress, protecting us from the difficulties we face in life (Ps 46:10). We need to let our limitations meet a limitless God.

My dual activities of pushing the boundaries of scientific knowledge in my field and teaching teenagers in my spare time helped me accept the place where my knowledge blurs and I see through a glass dimly. However, I also learned not to prematurely accept a limitation based on old scholarship or past experiences. My scientific net could capture valuable knowledge while still leaving room for spiritual truth to go undetected by natural means. I would need to wait for the answers to certain questions in life, but pursuing those answers kept my faith alive. I learned that even if I cannot overcome certain limits, I must possess both the courage to try and the grace to accept the outcome.

6

UNANSWERED QUESTIONS

Life is an unanswered question,
but let's still believe in the dignity
and importance of the question.

TENNESSEE WILLIAMS

"For my thoughts are not your thoughts,
neither are your ways my ways,"
declares the LORD.
"As the heavens are higher than the earth,
so are my ways higher than your ways
and my thoughts than your thoughts."

ISAIAH 55:8-9

FOR LEARNING EVERYTHING from multiplication tables to sight words, flashcards make a great teaching tool at the beginning of our education journeys. They also impart the subtle message that every question has a corresponding answer. Somewhere in the high school–level curriculum that paradigm begins to break down.

However, students retain the hope that future discoveries will provide the solutions to unanswered questions. At the college level, students realize that some questions may be unanswerable by their very nature.

Science seeks to push back the frontiers of knowledge. Scientists hope tomorrow's discoveries will replace today's unknowns. Yet some scientific discoveries remind us mysteries will remain. Some flashcards will have a blank on the other side.

In our personal lives, we construct narratives to process our experiences and help us find purpose and direction. Like a scientist altering a working hypothesis, we edit these stories as we gather more information and a better understanding. However, sometimes we face circumstances that make no sense, and life becomes as dissatisfying as reading a story with an undeveloped plot. How do we trust God when we have no answers? Can we deepen our faith in spite of our confusion? Is it possible to find peace in the midst of the unknown?

The Continuing Mystery

If uncertainty in our universe does not stop the advance of science, then uncertainty in our human lives need not hinder our journey of faith. Limits in life sometimes delay an answer beyond an individual's lifespan. Following a long list of heroes of the faith, Hebrews 11:39 states, "These were all commended for their faith, yet none of them received what had been promised."

Abraham counted the stars to fathom the number of his future descendants. He lived to see the birth of his son Isaac, but he never saw the day when his descendants were "as countless as the sand on the seashore" (Heb 11:12). Joseph looked forward to the time when the children of Israel would leave Egypt to journey to the Promised Land. As he was nearing death, he gave instructions for his bones to be carried to the Promised Land when God delivered Israel from Egypt

(Gen 50:24-25; Heb 11:22). When Moses led the children of Israel out of Egypt, he took the bones of Joseph with him (Ex 13:19). Joseph never lived to see the return to the Promised Land, but his bones followed the pillar of cloud by day and the pillar of fire by night through the desert along with the rest of Israel.

A long list of prophets, judges, kings and everyday people from Old Testament times looked forward to the coming of the Savior, understanding God's plan for salvation only in part while longing for more than they experienced in their lifetime. Those living after the birth of Christ know about the Savior in ways beyond the comprehension of the godly people from previous eras. However, those saints of old believed in the promise of a Savior by faith, content to live with many unanswered questions.

We learn from this long list of heroes of the faith found in Hebrews 11 that not all questions will be answered in our lifetime. Some promised dreams of God take multiple generations to fulfill. Like immigrants who leave their homeland in search of a better future for their children, our place in life may be to lay the groundwork for the generations to come.

Many founders of colleges and universities set in motion the institutions that have grown beyond their wildest dreams and also changed in ways beyond what they could fathom. However, the institutions are here today because of their faithful work shaping the future, past budget crises, tiny enrollment and difficulty recruiting professors and students.

When you encounter unanswered questions, consider the possibility that the answer may come outside the scope of your lifespan. If you feel you are headed in the right direction, keep going even when you can see the end result only by faith. Accept that every person will be left with mysteries that remain unsolved in that person's limited time on this planet. Faith brings the assurance that God is present even when his purposes remain hidden for the present time.

A quest for deeper understanding and greater knowledge is admirable. Just as scientists try to push back the boundaries of knowledge, scholars try to clarify the mysteries about the nature of God and how he operates within the universe. Study can help us find biblical support for concepts such as the Trinity, and we can devise helpful analogies to teach the concept to others. However, we will never fully understand how one divine nature is a unity of three distinct persons. Mystery is built into faith just as mystery is built into the universe.

Scientists who study the brain can map functions with increasing precision. Yet the leap from firing neurons to consciousness remains a mystery. Christians believe in the resurrection of the dead and the promise of eternal life. Yet when we try to understand how life can return to dry bones, we are left with the response of Ezekiel in the valley, "Sovereign LORD, you alone know" (Ezek 37:3).

Previous generations lived with greater ease alongside mystery. When people encountered strange diseases, they were comfortable explaining them as curses of the gods or punishments for evil. Now we look for bacteria, viruses, prions or altered physiology of cells to explain diseases. Instead of viewing droughts as a sign of a god's displeasure, we scan satellite images and measure atmospheric conditions to predict the weather. With many of the things once thought mysterious now explained by science, the current generation expects to make progress toward reducing the remaining mysteries.

Living in an era with good sanitation, I am grateful for those who discovered the relationship between bacteria and disease. Surgeons scrub up before entering the operating suite and save countless lives by preventing the transmission of infections. I hope medical science develops appropriate antibiotics to keep pace with the shifting mutations in bacterial strains. I look forward to a better understanding of conditions that create progressive cognitive decline, such as Alzheimer's disease, Lewy body disease and

Creutzfeldt-Jakob disease (CJD). I long to see many medical mysteries solved in my lifetime.

However, as much as the scientist in me hopes to reduce the presence of mysteries, I realize mysteries will remain. Research that succeeds in answering one question will open up several others. Some questions will belong at the intersection of science and theology, where both disciplines reach their limits. Thus, any answers to these questions will be partial at best.

Mystery is more than just a blank card waiting for a future answer. Mystery gives art its appeal. While science tries to define every variable and mark every boundary clearly, the beauty of art lies in the smudged lines, blended colors and ambiguous meaning of a painting. Take away the mystery, and you have a technical drawing or perhaps a cartoon.

Mystery makes it possible for two people to look at the same painting and walk away with different impressions about the significance and meaning of the work. The continuing mysteries in the universe and in the explanation of events in our lives work the same way. Two people can experience the same event, such as a natural disaster, and walk away with different spiritual interpretations. One person may see the hand of God in the comfort and peace found in the aftermath while the other recoils in horror at the possibility of God allowing such suffering to occur in the first place.

Mystery challenges us to continue to journey in faith despite remaining doubts. Parts of the painting of our lives might be crisp and clear while other areas fade and smear. In accepting that God's ways are superior to our own, we are deciding to embrace mystery and the possibility of unanswered questions in this lifetime. Recognizing the limits of our knowledge does not mean we give up on the dignity and importance of our questions. It just means we are ready to embrace our humanity.

THE UNWANTED DIAGNOSIS

Ready to depart on a long-awaited trip to Hawaii with his wife, a church elder heard the words no one wants to hear from his doctor, "We think it is cancer."

Ernie was the kind of man you could depend on, and everyone in his life did. He never lacked energy until after the cancer diagnosis. If you had a problem, you could call him up, and he'd make time to head your way with an offer of practical assistance.

In the days before we signed up for AAA membership, my husband locked his keys in the car in a garage in Boston. I had another set of car keys in our apartment but no means of transportation to the garage. In our small church, stories of this elder rescuing people from such situations were shared like legends. Part curious, part desperate and somewhat embarrassed, we reached out to see if he would drive the keys into Boston that evening. Although he was a well-known Christian leader throughout the New England area, no job was too small for him. He gave of his time that evening to rescue my husband from the garage in Boston, and he won our respect and gratitude in the process.

Ernie was no fool. His trip to Boston with a set of car keys was an investment he was making in the lives of a young couple. He understood better than anyone I have ever met how you earn the right to provide spiritual guidance for a person's life by taking action to show him you care about his needs. When he spoke, others listened because his deeds preceded his message.

After Ernie was diagnosed with cancer, he received prayers from people throughout New England. His church organized people to pray for him during a twenty-four-hour period, with each person signing up for a fifteen-minute segment. If the key to answered prayer rested in the sheer volume of the petitions rising to heaven, Ernie had no need to fear cancer. If the intensity of a person's own prayers determined whether the person received his request, Ernie could expect to hear from God. He trusted God would heal him and prayed daily toward that end. All those praying for him longed to see him minister once again and continue his service for God throughout the region. Ernie died of cancer less than a year after the unwanted diagnosis.

He left behind a large, grieving family and a heartbroken church. Thousands stood in line at the funeral home to pay their last respects to a remarkable man. I stood in line as well. While waiting, I heard stories echo up and down the line about how Ernie intervened at a crucial time in a person's life. Some talked of how he helped them find a job. Others talked of his wise advice. Most talked about how they came to faith in Jesus Christ because of Ernie's example.

Toward the end of his life when others asked in his presence why God could have allowed this disease in his life, Ernie invariably responded, "Why not me?" He knew better than to exempt himself from the sorrows one encounters in life. However, his funeral left many asking why. As with any question, one feels compelled to attempt an answer.

Maybe God taught us all a lesson about suffering with grace through Ernie's example at the end of his life. Like Job, he remained faithful to God throughout the entire ordeal. His passing prompted others to step up to the plate in the various ministries that now lacked his voice and his contributions. People previously dependent on this trustworthy man learned to become reliable themselves. All these answers ring of some truth.

However, Ernie's family knew certain questions would never be answered satisfactorily in this lifetime. To try to force an answer where none fits only disrespects the pain of those who grieve and dishonors the memory of the man. Sometimes "I don't know" is the most appropriate and kindest answer. Not all mysteries must be resolved. Letting the mysteries remain can be the most honest approach.

One of the mistakes of Job's friends was their rush to come up with neatly packaged answers to another person's pain. Job was one of the most prosperous men of his time, described in the Bible as "the greatest man among all the people of the East" (Job 1:3). He had a large family, a vast number of livestock and many servants.

Not only was Job prosperous, he was righteous. If there ever was a man who tried his best to follow all of God's laws, Job was the man. You might be tempted to draw a correlation between Job's spiritual life and his material blessings, and many did. The day came when God allowed Job to be tested. Job lost his possessions, his servants, and his seven sons and three daughters to multiple tragedies. Then Job lost his good health, and his body was covered with painful sores.

Now people were tempted to draw the reverse correlation between Job's spiritual life and his calamities. Even his three friends came to the conclusion that Job had sinned. Eliphaz, Bildad and Zophar initially did what good friends should do when someone is hurting. They showed up. Next, they sat in silence and gave him the gift of their presence without the clamor of words. They would have done well to venture no further. However, their next step was to do what many of us have done in similar circumstances—offer advice where none was needed.

The first friend to speak was Eliphaz. In response to Job's lament, he replied,

> If someone ventures a word with you, will you be impatient?
> But who can keep from speaking? (Job 4:2)

When comforting a friend experiencing loss and tragedy, the restraint to "keep from speaking" can be the best gift you offer. However, Eliphaz could not resist the opportunity to instruct the instructor, to counsel the counselor and to place the blame for these tragedies at the feet of Job.

While Eliphaz said good things about the need to turn to God and pray for relief, his message only brought Job more sorrow. Now to all his other losses Job could add the loss of his friends' belief in his integrity. When ministering to someone who has suffered hardship, consider the lesson of Eliphaz. Resist the urge to offer solutions to imagined problems. Do more listening than speaking. Realize your presence is more valuable than your advice.

The next friend to share his thoughts with Job was Bildad. Bildad offered sound theology about the just nature of God. He exhorted Job to trust that God would restore him and clothe Job's enemies in shame. Job acknowledged that Bildad's words were true. However, Job knew from experience that life cannot be tied up into a neat theological bow. Suffering comes to both the righteous and the wicked. Furthermore, no one is truly righteous and able to stand before a holy God without an arbitrator, or Savior.

The lesson from Bildad is to avoid offering someone a simple answer to a complicated problem. Bildad's words rang true in the long run; God gave Job a double portion of all he had before his tragedies. In the rush to comfort someone, we can make the mistake of skipping past the messy aspects of life to get to the happy ending. Real life does not proceed in a straight line from trouble to resolution. Each person must make the journey through sorrow on that person's own timetable. We can offer encouragement, but we should not expect people to alter their emotions until they are ready. Job needed to work through his frustrations and his sadness before he moved to hope and confidence.

Zophar weighed in with his take on Job's situation after the two other friends had spoken. He treated Job as if he were an arrogant man who needed to repent of his sins to regain God's blessings. While Zophar upheld the omnipotence and justice of God, he showed no compassion to his friend. You can hear a tinge of smugness

in Zophar's tone. He is feeling superior to Job as he lectures him on
the power of God.

Job had the perfect response to all three of his friends.

> Doubtless you are the only people,
>   and wisdom will die with you!
> But I have a mind as well as you;
>   I am not inferior to you.
> Who does not know all these things?
> I have become a laughingstock to my friends,
>   though I called upon God and he answered—
>   a mere laughingstock, though righteous and blameless!
> Those who are at ease have contempt for misfortune
>   as the fate of those whose feet are slipping. (Job 12:2-5)

Do not make the mistake of despising someone going through a
challenge, whose dreams appear to have turned into nightmares. Job
teaches us the foolishness of such thinking. God is just. He blesses his
children. But he never promised life would be so simple. Today you
may lecture your friend. Tomorrow you may suffer.

Sorrow happens. God is faithful. Both truths work together in the
life of a person facing unanswered questions. There are times in life
when a person boards the plane for a vacation in Hawaii, enjoying
seemingly undeserved blessings. There may also be the time of an
unwanted diagnosis, when a person faces seemingly undeserved
hardship. God is present in both the celebration and the suffering. A
good friend will learn to be present as well, letting go of the need for
answers to the why questions and exploring the possibilities in the
now-what questions. When we move beyond seeking to explain suffering, we can concentrate on responding to suffering as God's agents
of healing and compassion in the lives of those affected by tragedies.
We can become an answer to someone's prayer.

THE CLOSED DOOR

We experience spiritual growth in those moments when our hearts are broken and our minds remain unsatisfied, yet our faith rises above the uncertainty to provide strength and peace. Sometimes the unanswered questions involve not hardships but simply a closed door.

As an undergraduate, I planned to stay in Pennsylvania for both my undergraduate and graduate studies. However, when the only professor involved in the type of cancer research that interested me left for another university, I faced a closed door. At the time, the closed door was a frustration and a complication in my life.

Of course, all my adventures in New England were born from this closed door. The opportunity to get my doctorate from Harvard University and work in a wonderful collaborative research group came my way when I turned from the closed door and headed in a fresh direction. The friends I made, the home I established and my children's experiences in Massachusetts are all a result of that closed door.

I would not want to change the good things that came from my move to Boston although I wanted to change the closed door when I first encountered it. My perspective on the closed door changed with time. From the day I learned the unpleasant news to the moment the closed door finally started making sense to me, I had to live with unanswered questions.

Those encountering closed doors often find comfort in the words from Jeremiah 29:11, "'For I know the plans I have for you,' declares the LORD, 'plans to prosper you and not to harm you, plans to give you hope and a future.'" Of course, those comforting words come right after the verse that says, "When seventy years are completed for Babylon, I will come to you and fulfill my good promise to bring you back to this place" (Jer 29:10).

The people who lived in Jerusalem were carried away captive into Babylon by Nebuchadnezzar, a conqueror. False prophets tried to comfort them with the thought that their exile would be short-lived. However, God intended for the period of exile to last seventy years.

This plan was not what the people wanted. However, it was in their best interest to accept their new reality. God sent a message to the exiles through the prophet Jeremiah:

> Build houses and settle down; plant gardens and eat what they produce. Marry and have sons and daughters; find wives for your sons and give your daughters in marriage, so that they too may have sons and daughters. Increase in number there; do not decrease. Also, seek the peace and prosperity of the city to which I have carried you into exile. Pray to the LORD for it, because if it prospers, you too will prosper. (Jer 29:5-7)

The people needed to know they should live their lives as if they were going to be exiled in Babylon for a couple of generations. The sooner they accepted the closed door for their quick return to Jerusalem, the sooner they could turn to the business of establishing themselves in Babylon. Trying to leave a place where God intended them to be for a season would be counterproductive. The people needed to seek the peace and prosperity of Babylon, for their own welfare would be tied to the prosperity of this city.

These verses form the context for the well-known promise in Jeremiah 29:11. God's plans to prosper his people and give them hope were tied to their ability to come to peace with their closed door. In seventy years, God would open that door again for another generation, but these people needed to live with their unanswered questions and trust God with their unfulfilled dreams.

Sometimes you need to push against a closed door, but other times, like the exiles from Jerusalem to Babylon, you need to accept redirection. If the passage of time or your own actions can open the door, keep trying. Otherwise, prepare to move on. Perhaps a high school student receives a rejection letter from the college of his choice. A young adult may be unable to find the right job in a city where she wants to live. A company may downsize, forcing a family to relocate. In these situations, happiness returns when a person shifts gears and embraces change.

Intellectually, I understand the importance of change, but I have never been a fan of unwanted change in my life. I am more suited for situations that demand patience and perseverance than ones that require a quick shift in plans. However, life requires both skills.

Turning from a closed door requires the active process of seeking a new open door. Here, perseverance has its place. "Ask and it will be given to you; seek and you will find; knock and the door will be opened to you. For everyone who asks receives; the one who seeks finds; and to the one who knocks, the door will be opened" (Mt 7:7-8). The exiles needed to engage in life and build families in Babylon. Their orders from heaven were to increase and not decrease.

I believe God wants every person who faces a closed door to embrace the challenge to increase and not decrease. See the ending of one season in your life as the chance to prune away the parts of your life that no longer work for your future. The pruning may result in a temporary decrease in branches, but the end result should be as it is in nature: the pruning should increase the fruitfulness of the branches that remain.

I could not stay in Pennsylvania and also build a new life in Boston. I needed to leave familiar places and customs behind and let valued friendships wane. When I first moved to New England, both the winters and the people seemed a little colder than the ones in Pennsylvania. In my experience growing up in Pittsburgh, the city with a smile on its face, strangers would strike up conversations with one another in the supermarket. In Boston, people seemed more focused on attending to the business at hand. I learned that New Englanders make loyal friends once you get to know them, but I experienced a bit of an adjustment period during my first year in Boston.

I think one good way to move on after a closed door is to suspend judgment for a while after the experience. If the closed door involves loss, then a time of grief may be in order. In Psalm 137, we see the emotional response of the exiles in Babylon.

> By the rivers of Babylon we sat down and wept
>   when we remembered Zion. (Ps 137:1)

Although God wanted the people to establish themselves and work toward the prosperity of their new home, their sorrow at their loss of their homeland was appropriate.

However, for us to fully embrace the promise of God to prosper us in new circumstances, we need to find peace in the gap between the intensity of our initial grief and our eventual acceptance of God's plan to give us a future where he has placed us. When we come to terms with God's sovereignty in our lives, then we will be willing to accept that his ways are wiser than our own. We will be able to trust him even when we do not have the answer.

For a researcher, a closed door in a line of scientific experimentation can feel like a loss of time and money. However, learning what does not work is part of the process of finding what does work. Thomas Edison needed to test many different filaments before finding the one that worked best in the light bulb. In the pharmaceutical industry, thousands of compounds are tested in hopes of finding a few with the right active properties. In the days before more direct genetic manipulation through recombinant DNA technology, researchers would screen thousands of mutations looking for the one with the desired characteristics.

In life, we will experience dead ends as means of redirection. If we consider each closed door to be bringing us closer to the correct door, we will be able to persevere and move past our momentary discouragement. The unresolved questions will not keep us from continuing to trust God as we move into an uncertain future. Living with mysteries will not disturb our confidence. We will flip through the stack of flashcards and merely shrug when we see one with a blank for an answer.

7

Doubts Born from Pain

Pain is the question mark turned like
a fishhook in the human heart.

PETER DE VRIES

Consider it pure joy, my brothers and sisters,
whenever you face trials of many kinds,
because you know that the testing of
your faith develops perseverance.

JAMES 1:2-3

LONG AGO, BEFORE THE INVENTION of the fire hose, towns-people would work together to put out fires by lining up from the water well to the fire so they could pass buckets of water down the line to douse the fire quickly. The bucket brigade may be an image of the past, but many modern processes involve similar teamwork.

Many medical advances that impact treatment of patients travel down the line from basic research on cells to verification in animal models to tests in a series of clinical trials on human subjects. No one researcher or research group handles the entire process, which is often spread across decades. Basic cancer researchers trying to understand growth mechanisms in cells dream that their findings will prompt further research that will eventually lead to a clinical trial. Medical doctors conducting clinical trials hope basic researchers will find new compounds or treatment options worth testing in clinical trials.

My involvement in cancer research was at the beginning of the bucket brigade. I thought about genes, DNA, RNA, protein and cellular processes. Things are complicated at this level, but not nearly as complicated as the treatment of patients. Patients have minds of their own and may not be compliant with treatment. Even the best science cannot help a patient who withdraws from medical care.

Patients refuse treatment for a number of reasons, including fear of the pain involved in a procedure. Sometimes the burden of a certain treatment, such as a type of chemotherapy, seems worse than the disease. In the early stages, many types of cancer have few or no symptoms. Thus, the treatment seems to create problems rather than solve them. Of course, if the consequence of forgoing treatment is death, then the burden of the treatment may be justified.

In our spiritual lives, we can seek to avoid the pain that comes with personal growth, behaving like difficult patients. When pain occurs, we may see the greater good at work in our lives, like a child enduring the pain of vaccination in order to avoid the possibility of a debilitating disease. We may also respond to pain by withdrawing and allowing our questions to turn like fishhooks into our hearts. While intellectual doubts can become stumbling blocks to faith, doubts born of pain can do even greater damage to our relationship with God and others if they go unaddressed. Like a spiritual cancer, these doubts need treatment, although the procedure may produce more pain in the short run.

FAITH TESTED IN SUFFERING

Whenever a friend or acquaintance of mine received a cancer diagnosis, I stepped beyond my world of cancer cells to think about the disease in terms of patients. I thought about clinical trials from the perspective of a patient deciding whether to enroll. I read articles about alternative treatments with an open mind. I considered how a patient would view a certain treatment option. I thought about how cancer impacts the family of the patient.

When both of my parents were diagnosed with different types of cancer within two weeks of each other, it felt like cancer had invaded every waking hour of my life. In the evening, I prepared cancer cells in the tissue culture hood for the next day's experiment. Late at night, I would research information related to my parents' illnesses, then catch some sleep to be ready for a long day at the lab bench. Months passed in a blur of total immersion in the topic of cancer.

On an emotional and physical level, the experience was intense and exhausting. However, on an intellectual level, the journey was stimulating and fruitful. Reading about various chemotherapeutic treatments made me consider the value of a certain chemotherapeutic compound in the design of one of my crucial experiments. I also considered using cancer cells with different properties in my work.

Spiritually, you may know many Scripture verses about God's faithfulness and promises, but when pain comes into your life, your faith meets reality. Nothing is theoretical anymore. James tells us we should "consider it pure joy" when we face trials because the testing of our faith helps us develop perseverance (Jas 1:2-3).

An endurance runner starts out running a relatively short distance and then lengthens his run in practice sessions. By the time race day arrives, he can complete the full course without difficulty. In the same way, experiences that stretch our faith and push the limits of our spiritual endurance can make us stronger believers. Of course, if we approach these experiences incorrectly, we can walk away with injuries.

Not all agnostics and atheists come to their beliefs through difficult circumstances, but many have lost their faith through doubts born from pain. Peter De Vries, raised as a Calvinist and trained at Calvin College in Grand Rapids, Michigan, published in 1961 a well-known novel titled *The Blood of the Lamb,* about a man losing his faith in a benevolent God after a series of losses in his life. One of those losses echoed the real-life loss of Peter De Vries's ten-year-old daughter, Emily, to leukemia in 1960 after a two-year battle with the disease. Peter De Vries became a famous atheist because the pain of his daughter's death became a question mark turned into a fishhook in his own heart.

The apostle Peter urged believers in Asia Minor who were undergoing persecution to stay strong in spite of suffering. In 1 Peter 4:12-13, he offered these words of encouragement: "Dear friends, do not be surprised at the fiery ordeal that has come to you to test you, as though something strange were happening to you. But rejoice inasmuch as you participate in the sufferings of Christ, so that you may be overjoyed when his glory is revealed." Peter's advice can be extended to all believers experiencing shocking life circumstances.

The danger to faith when things seem to go wrong in a believer's life comes from the wrong view of God. If you view God as a protective parent who will keep you from falling and scraping your spiritual knees, you will feel unloved and abandoned when life brings injury. If you view prayer as a magic formula to make your desires come true, your faith will hit a brick wall when things don't turn out according to your plans. If you view life on a short horizon, you will see only the pain and not the fruit that comes from perseverance.

For these reasons, Peter wanted believers not to be surprised when painful trials came into their life. He wanted them to be prepared for the rainy days as well as the sunshine. Faith was not only for times when the believers sang uplifting songs of worship together. Faith needed to work when the believers were scattered, alone and afraid, facing persecution under the reign of Nero in Rome. Peter knew persecution could unsettle the faith of many of the believers who expected God to protect them from the atrocities committed by an evil ruler such as Nero. He wanted them to have a mature understanding of suffering so their faith would not be shaken.

Peter tied together the concepts of sufferings and glory, an unlikely pair. Believers build their Christian faith on the resurrection power of Christ. The crowds followed Jesus to witness and experience his healing touch and see miraculous signs. However, Peter wrote of the value of participating in the sufferings of Christ. The cross is a revered symbol of God's forgiveness made possible through the sacrifice of Jesus. Many people will gladly accept the offer of salvation symbolized by the cross, but only a few willingly embrace the self-denial inherent in the message of the cross.

Peter called believers not only to accept the possibility of suffering but also to rejoice in the opportunity. Enduring the trials brings the glory. Only when your soul has experienced the bleakness of a dark night do you appreciate the gift of the light penetrating your despair. When you hold no further illusions about your own strength, you can see God's sustaining power at work. When the heaviness of suffering lifts, your joy overflows.

Unlike an athlete who experiences the glory of victory as the end result of suffering through training and physical exertion, the believer experiences the revealing not of his own glory but of the glory of Christ. Suffering reveals a believer's limits and increases his reliance on others and his dependence on God. Thus, the very experience that shows a person his weakness turns out to reveal the strength he has through faith. Paul spoke of the same process: "Therefore I will boast all the more gladly about my weaknesses, so that Christ's power may rest on me. That is why, for Christ's sake, I delight in weaknesses, in insults, in hardships, in persecution, in difficulties. For when I am weak, then I am strong" (2 Cor 12:9-10).

The rigors of reality should not dissipate a person's faith, just as immersion in the topic of cancer did not make me weary of the subject. Any faith worth having must be built to handle the vicissitudes of life. The key to getting through a trial is to jettison false notions about God, life and the human condition and to trust even in those moments when you cannot understand.

FEAR WRAPPED IN FAITH

"Perfect love drives out fear" (1 Jn 4:18), making fear and love opposite sides of a coin. Paul said, "If I have a faith that can move mountains, but do not have love, I am nothing" (1 Cor 13:2). While mature faith leads to love, Paul considered it theoretically possible to have faith without love. While fear and faith appear to contradict each other, sometimes they coexist, dancing together like courage and fear.

My mother feared cancer like no other disease because of her experience as a young adult watching her father die from lung cancer. She knew he prayed no family member would ever suffer from the disease, and she trusted that prayer would protect her from a cancer diagnosis. When she experienced troubling symptoms that hinted at the possibility of uterine cancer, she wrapped her fears in a false layer of faith. Real faith places trust in the sovereignty of God, abandoning itself to the phrase Jesus spoke at Gethsemane, "not what I will, but what you will" (Mk 14:36).

Counterfeit faith quotes all the right Scriptures with the appropriate spiritual tone but makes room for only one answer. This faith represents hope for a desired outcome, but not necessarily trust in an omnipotent God. In my mother's case, her faith was sincere, but it was a blanket to wrap around her fears instead of a force to vanquish them.

When she was a young girl, she made her first trip to the hospital in the middle of the night with an appendix ready to burst. The doctors who performed the emergency surgery used clamps to close her incision. The removal of those clamps was painful, and she associated hospitals with negative experiences. Although her stay in the hospital prolonged her life for nearly six more decades, she grew up in an era when many of her family members believed that hospitals were places you went into sick and came out dead. So she refused to return to the doctor to confirm her cancer diagnosis and proceed with the necessary treatment.

Her faith did not help her because it served as a crutch to keep her from facing her need for medical treatment as her symptoms grew worse. While I wanted to support her decision, I needed to be sure she understood the choice she was making. As a cancer researcher, I represented the reality she did not want to face, so she decided to limit her contact with me in the months preceding her death.

Cancer treatments require that the patient fight to survive and draw upon emotional reserves to endure the experience. While I might consider forcing a patient to set a broken bone against his will, I could not force my mother to undergo an experience that she would resist with her whole being. Any treatment she would receive had no guarantee of success. While I thought she was making a dangerous decision, I respected her right to decide how to proceed.

My father underwent radiation treatment for stage IV head and neck cancer. He then underwent surgery to be sure all the cancer was gone. When the doctors performed the surgery, they found no re-maining cancer. His story was a combination medical miracle and answer to prayer. His recovery was part encouragement for my mother to hope for a healing and part cautionary tale. After all, medical treatment was part of his miracle. My father gave God the option of working either through medicine or through a miracle. The end result was a complete recovery.

My father believed if only one in a million people recovered from his type of cancer, he would be that one in a million. He had faith but sounded far less spiritual than my mother. He had fear mixed with faith, but the faith permeated the fear and subdued it. Fortunately, the return of his health enabled him to serve as a caretaker for my mother. Like her father, my mother walked around in relatively good health up to the end of her life. She died peacefully in her sleep forty-three years after the death of her father. A few days before her death, she expressed regret at not undergoing medical treatment for her cancer. Strangely, this admission brought me peace in the days to follow. Within her last few days on earth, she embraced a more solid faith. This faith did not grant her wish, but it sustained her for the final steps on her journey. She understood that the outcome of her disease was the product of her decision and not the failure of God to hear her prayers.

Her peaceful death attested to a faith greater than one that brings about a desired result. Her journey was over, and she knew the Savior. She found a healing deeper than a temporal healing from cancer. While treatment may have prolonged her days, her life was in no way incomplete.

RESOLUTION FOUND IN FORGIVENESS

While my mother's death filled me with grief, I also experienced a resolution of my feelings. I chose to have her laid to rest in a pink silk dress I had purchased for her when we went shopping together in happier times. My father and I made preparations for a funeral in accordance with her wishes. I chose not to place blame on God, church or faith for the outcome of my mother's illness. I understood that she had a genuine Christian faith but clung to an error in one area of her life. In her final months many people, including a pastor in the Pittsburgh area, tried to persuade her to see treatment as an extension of her faith. Unfortunately, she placed her trust in teachings without a good balance between faith and reason from programs on Christian radio stations.

The pastor knew my mother and understood her situation. The teachers on the radio played into my mother's fears while bolstering her spiritual pride. They did her a disservice and created a barrier between her and the wise words from her concerned family. Ultimately, my mother bore responsibility for her choices, but some culpability rests with the false teachers who set her up for spiritual failure.

I decided to create a moment for myself at the end of her funeral where I would release myself from the negative impact of my mother's death. After taking care of all the aspects of the service and greeting the guests, after everyone else started walking to their cars, I would place a single rose on my mother's casket. The rose would represent my offer of forgiveness to my mother for her negative actions toward me as she clung to a flawed faith to avoid facing her fears. Leaving the rose behind on top of the casket would represent my decision to leave the pain of this experience in the past where it could not harm my future or my feelings toward the church at large for harboring such false teachings.

When the moment came at the end of the funeral, I followed through with my plan. I felt peace flood my heart as I walked away from my mother for the last time. I headed back to my parents' home with my father and husband, prepared to feed a small army of relatives for the wake. As an only child, I had much to do. When the last guest left the house, I broke down in the sobs of grief that can flow freely after finishing all responsibilities. My grief did not include anger at God, for my pain remained at the cemetery with the single rose.

My father's faith never fully recovered from my mother's death. He lived another twelve and a half years, but his distaste for organized religion lived with him. He continued to believe in God but resented the teachings that cut his wife's life short. The experience of her death became his excuse for stunted spiritual growth and lack of church participation. He did not suffer from cancer, but he suffered from doubts born from pain.

My mother's death illustrated the danger of separation between the riverbanks of faith and reasoning. She felt that denying logic was a measure of the strength of her faith. In reality, she weakened her faith in the sovereignty of God by limiting the means of potential healing. Although she hoped her actions would strengthen the faith of others, in the end, they became a stumbling block.

I do believe God's grace was greater than the errors she was taught, but my family paid a price for false teaching. She never lived to see her grandchildren, while my father did. We all missed her presence in our lives.

Paul told the believers who lived in Rome, "We know that in all things God works for the good of those who love him, who have been called according to his purpose" (Rom 8:28). If I look for the good that emerged as a result of my mother's experience, I find my own deepened commitment to help people integrate faith and science. For individuals like my mother, a heavy-handed medical approach that disrespects their faith simply scares them away. Whatever positive contribution medicine could make in their lives is lost.

On the other hand, a world of faith that mocks the advances of science breeds spiritual arrogance and plants the seeds of destruction in the lives of vulnerable people. Humility on both of the riverbanks builds the bridge that helps people. I am grateful for medical programs that teach future doctors to respect the faiths of their patients while also guiding the patients in productive directions for their physical health. Similarly, I appreciate pastors and chaplains who know how to partner with doctors to address the spiritual and emotional needs of people without discrediting the advice of the medical profession.

While the science behind medical treatment is precise, the art of bringing healing to human beings is inexact. Sometimes patients who receive the best medical care still die. Other times, patients experience spontaneous remissions that leave science grasping for explanations and people of faith declaring a miracle. Pain occurring on the physical level needs spiritual treatment as well as medical treatment. Care of the whole patient—body, mind and spirit—may be the best way to prevent and treat doubts born from pain.

A partnership between those who care for spiritual needs and those who care for physical needs provides total care for patients and their families. While medical professionals must take a scientific view of patients' medical conditions, an open mind toward the contribution of a patient's spiritual health and cultural beliefs can create trust between the patient and the medical establishment. Patients who feel understood and supported are better able to endure difficult treatments and retain the will to fight for survival.

While I returned to the laboratory after my mother's death to continue basic research related to cancer, I gained a greater appreciation for the complications that occur at the bedside. I appreciated on a new level the limits of science and the dangers of faith without reasoning. My faith grew to embrace a sovereign God with the freedom to answer prayers in ways beyond our understanding. I moved past doubts born from pain but grew to empathize with believers working through the difficult questions that can become fishhooks in our hearts.

8

DISILLUSIONMENT MASQUERADING AS DOUBT

We can destroy ourselves by cynicism and disillusion,
just as effectively as by bombs.

KENNETH CLARK

But as for me, my feet had almost slipped;
I had nearly lost my foothold.
For I envied the arrogant
when I saw the prosperity of the wicked.

PSALM 73:2-3

NOT ALL DOUBTS ORIGINATE IN THE MIND; some emanate from the heart. Jesus set a high standard for Christian relationships, giving his followers a new commandment, "Love one another. As I have loved you, so you must love one another. By this everyone will know that you are my disciples, if you love one another" (Jn 13:34-35). Obedience to this commandment provides the most powerful Christian apologetic available.

Anyone who has spent a few years in a church environment can tell you a story of the pain experienced when this commandment is broken. George Santayana, the Spanish American philosopher, poet and Harvard professor, once said, "Wisdom comes by disillusionment." The word *disillusionment* means a loss of illusions. Illusions are distortions of reality, errors in perception. Surely, being set free from a distorted view of reality must be in a person's best interest. When difficult and painful experiences reveal a more accurate and mature portrait of life, wisdom increases.

Yet illusions bring comfort. When people walk through the front door of a church, they reach for the promise of heaven on earth. They yearn for a warm, extended spiritual family capable of providing security and a genuine sense of belonging. They expect church leaders and fellow believers to meet their needs, value their opinions and embrace their talents. They hope people receiving their ministry will overlook their faults and admire their strengths.

Illusions flourish beyond the church in work environments, educational settings and relationships. Dream jobs can become nightmares with long hours, jealous coworkers and career dead ends. Education can open a person's eyes to the overwhelming amount of injustice, poverty and violence in the world, creating discontent and raising questions about the goodness of God. Strains in human relationships can lead to strain in a person's relationship with God when a person faces the frustration of unmet expectations.

When life experiences shatter our comforting illusions, we have an opportunity to gain wisdom. However, in such difficult moments we may purchase a false perception of reality at a steep spiritual price. Instead of adjusting our focus to see the truth more clearly, we can allow our disappointment to obscure our vision. Doubt settles like a fog as we stand surrounded by the shards of our illusions. Confused by the clouds of our emotions, we mistake cynicism for wisdom. We rightfully ask questions, but the wrong ones. We arrive at conclusions far from our destination.

I believe we should welcome the disillusionment that sets us free from our naiveté but shun the cynicism that strips us of faith itself. When our hearts are filled with doubt, we must ask ourselves if this doubt is simply the product of disillusionment. Throughout my years in church, I have witnessed believers going through disillusioning experiences. In addition, I have heard stories of such experiences recalled in vivid detail years after the event. What do you tell the young man who thought he heard God tell him whom he was to marry, only to find himself rejected by the promised young woman? How do you restore the confidence of a wounded associate minister who trusted a flawed senior leader? What words will console the pastor of many years' standing whose congregation divided in a church split? What explanation do you offer to the college student who wonders why society appears indifferent to the injustice in the world? Wisdom waits at the end of the journey through disillusionment, but no one looks forward to making the trip.

IMPERFECTIONS AND THE IDEAL

Most of my life I have lived just outside a city, deriving comfort from the availability of amenities within the city even if I seldom explored those resources. Just knowing that museums, stadiums and city lights exist beyond a short drive and a bridge makes me content. However, proximity to a city means the night sky glows with background light that obscures the presence of many stars. I never appreciated how magnificent the night sky could be until one night during my undergraduate years when I was walking along a country road after a gathering at a professor's house in the middle of a vast stretch of Pennsylvania farmland eleven miles from Penn State University. On this December evening, the only lights from civilization were tiny candles in the

windows of the farmhouses. The sky looked like the black velvet that
lines jewelry boxes. The stars shone with the clarity of diamonds, thousands of them tumbling from a vast heavenly treasure chest. Alone in
silence with my thoughts except for the snow crunching under my feet
and the occasional bark from the dog I had volunteered to walk that
night, I came to a richer appreciation of the verse from Psalm 19,

> The heavens declare the glory of God;
>   the skies proclaim the work of his hands. (Ps 19:1)

Since I was engaged and planning a spring wedding, perhaps the
imagery of diamonds best fits my memories of that night. The possibilities for my future seemed as limitless as the expanse of stars
overhead. I did not know then that my impression of the night sky on
that winter evening would provide wisdom for approaching disillusioning experiences many times in the years to follow.

In the years since that night, I have seen and experienced circumstances that highlight the imperfections of humanity. I have wondered
how churches can divide into political factions and lose sight of their
original mission. I have seen followers of Christ gossip about one
another, demonstrate insensitivity, allow discrimination and condone
thoughtless behavior. In my darkest moments of despair, appalled by
the conduct I witnessed in the lives of those who called themselves
Christians, I teetered on the brink of questioning God's presence and
ability to change human lives.

Ultimately, I wrestled with the question, should I expect more of
Christ's followers than of those who profess no such faith? I discovered the inescapable biblical answer is yes! Those who follow
Christ are the salt of the earth, as Jesus himself explained during his
Sermon on the Mount. Salt that loses its savor is cast aside. Jesus instructed his followers to "let your light shine before others, that they
may see your good deeds and glorify your Father in heaven" (Mt 5:16).

In Matthew 5:48, Jesus himself sets high expectations for his followers: "Be perfect, therefore, as your heavenly Father is perfect." Thus, we should expect more of those who claim to follow him. If we choose to follow him, we should expect more of ourselves. In the midst of human imperfections, including our own, we must not lose sight of the ideal. On a stormy night in the city, you will see no stars in the sky, only gray, billowing clouds and a background haze of city light. What a contrast from a walk on a country road on a cold, clear night! The stars still shine on stormy nights in the city, even if they are obscured, just as God's ideals remain in the midst of human imperfections.

I believe God put the stars in the sky so we can reach for them. When I see those innumerable stars glowing in the vast sky above me, I remember how "the heavens declare the glory of God" (Ps 19:1). Human beings will "fall short of the glory of God" (Rom 3:23), but the stars remind me to keep reaching toward God's standards. No one is righteous (Rom 3:10). Everyone needs a Savior. The imperfections I see in church culture and within individual Christians, including myself, point me back to the truth of the gospel message. Unfortunately, when others around us fall short of God's standards, they may hurt us in the process. Human failure, however, does not become an excuse for lowering the standards and losing sight of the stars.

Someone else's failure cannot become my excuse. I can choose to forgive even if I never hear an apology from the person who caused me harm. I can keep my heart tender. I can walk across the room to greet someone who has not done right by me, offering him or her a gift of grace. Those who love gazing at the stars understand the importance of grace. If I choose to turn my back or walk in the opposite direction, gray clouds gather in the skies overhead, obscuring my view of the glory of God.

In emphasizing the value of forgiveness, I do not want to trivialize anyone's disillusioning experience. These situations break the heart of

God. For example, God does not look kindly on leaders who harm his people. Ezekiel 34:2-10 describes God's judgment on the leaders of Israel who were like bad shepherds who did not care for the sheep. God promised in Ezekiel 34:10 to hold self-serving leaders accountable for not properly tending his flock, eventually removing them from positions of leadership. Moreover, he promised to rescue the sheep and take care of their needs himself. He states in Ezekiel 34:16, "I will shepherd the flock with justice." Leaders who intentionally hurt followers ultimately will answer to God. However, failed leaders need not be an excuse for failed followers. In promising to care for the flock that has been neglected and scattered through poor leadership, followers find a promise that God will make a way for them in the midst of a bad situation. When human leadership has brought disappointment, Christians can place their trust in God's leadership.

Furthermore, if you feel that there has been no justice in your particular situation, remember that the purest form of justice often takes years to unfold. One challenge you will face in the aftermath of a disillusioning experience is the temptation to believe the lie that nothing really matters after all. Those who envy "the prosperity of the wicked" (Ps 73:3) begin to forget that God still "rewards those who earnestly seek him" (Heb 11:6). Disillusionment can cause you to miss all the good around you as you focus on the few who have disappointed you. Yet time has a way of putting all life experiences into proper perspective.

DANGER IN A PENDULUM'S SWING

While serving as a youth leader within my local church, I loved to take students on a field trip to the Boston Museum of Science. The event was a practical way I could bridge the world of faith and science in the lives of my students. The highlight of the field trip came after an hour or so of wandering through the many intriguing exhibits. My husband and I would gather the students for an excursion to the gift shop. Selecting a gift was like picking which part of the museum you wanted to take home with you. From colorful geodes to elaborate science kits, there was something for everyone in every price range. After shopping, the students would meet outside the gift shop in the main lobby near the display of a Foucault pendulum. This pendulum reminded me of a similar display in the Buhl Science Center in Pittsburgh that I found fascinating in my own youth. The five-story-high pendulum, which demonstrates the earth's rotation, drew the interest of my students as well.

Each morning the museum staff starts the motion of the heavy pendulum and places a series of steel pins on the disc underneath the pendulum. Each steel pin marks an hour of the day from museum opening to museum closing. The pendulum swings in the same vertical plane as the earth rotates beneath it. Every hour the pendulum knocks down a steel pin, marking the rotation of the earth as the day progresses. The French physicist Jean Bernard Léon Foucault invented the first such demonstration of the earth's rotation in 1851, installing a pendulum in the Paris Observatory. A few weeks later, Foucault constructed his most famous pendulum in the dome of the Panthéon in Paris by suspending a 28-kilogram brass-coated lead bob from a 67-meter wire. The popularity of the display resulted in the installation of many Foucault pendulums in universities, science museums and planetariums around the world. Nearly 150 years after Foucault built his first pendulum, my youth group and I were enjoying the fruits of his ingenuity.

My students found something mesmerizing about the motion of the pendulum. Once the museum staff pulled the pendulum to one side and released it, the pendulum would oscillate from one side to the other for a very long time before eventually coming to rest in the center of the disc. In addition to demonstrating the reality of the earth's rotation, the Foucault pendulum also illustrates a potential spiritual danger a person faces after going through a disillusioning experience.

Sometimes a disillusioning experience is the clearest path back to spiritual wholeness. If all goes well in a person's life, the person may never see the truth that would free them from an unhealthy situation. Of course, a person who begins to see the truth enters a difficult transition season. Just as a pendulum pulled to one side then released will swing all the way to the other side, a person coming out of a disillusioning experience is in danger of letting go of his faith entirely. A person may need to be stripped of the false illusions created in an environment of error and misperceptions, but wholeness comes when the pendulum returns to center.

Believers who join unhealthy churches may find themselves gradually shifting from worshiping Christ to worshiping the human leaders. Those leaders can promote unbiblical teachings that trap their followers into the bondage of excessive legalism. In addition to following a long list of dos and don'ts, the followers can find that leaders seek to control their lives in unhealthy ways. The leaders might alienate believers from their families, discouraging believers from visiting their relatives. Participation in church activities might exclude other healthy pursuits in a person's life. The church leader may try to control decisions about marriage, career and education in the life of the follower. The church might promote the refusal of medical care in the name of faith.

In certain instances, churches can become spiritually and emotionally unhealthy for certain families while remaining healthy for the majority of the membership. For example, individuals within the leader's inner circle may be exposed to a dark side of the leader's personality. The leader may be controlling toward highly involved church members, displaying anger that seems completely out of character with the warm, friendly persona that most church members experience from the leader on Sunday mornings. As a result, the families experiencing emotional or spiritual abuse may feel isolated from the rest of the congregation, realizing that few within the church will believe them if they decide to express their concerns.

Breaking free from an unhealthy church is essential for regaining spiritual well-being. However, the goal for the individual or family walking away from a negative church experience is to reestablish balance in their spiritual life. The prescription for restoring and maintaining spiritual health is to check all teachings against Scripture, to connect with the wider Christian community by talking with friends in other churches and by consulting wise counselors, and to learn from the historical Christian community by reading commentaries and theological writings. The Bible describes in the early church a wonderful group of believers called the Bereans. Acts 17:11 tells us, "Now the Berean Jews were of more noble character than those in Thessalonica, for they received the message with great eagerness and examined the Scriptures every day to see if what Paul said was true." The Bereans were not a difficult group of believers that gave their spiritual leader a hard time. They were eager to hear the message that the apostle Paul delivered to them. However, they wisely checked everything that Paul said against the truth of the Scriptures. All good pastors will rejoice if you tell them that after hearing their sermons on Sunday morning you go home and check the messages against your Bible.

Some churches have doctrinally sound teachings and express good beliefs, appearing healthy and inviting to visitors walking through their doors. However, in spite of saying all the right words, the people within the church may not be living out what they believe. A person who becomes more involved may find a toxic environment created by abusive or unhealthy relationships or power struggles within the church leadership ranks.

Unfortunately, a person's ability to understand and apply biblical concepts may be skewed as a result of harm done by others. Like the pendulum that will not come to rest at the center until swinging back and forth for a long time, a person may need time to rebuild trust and absorb correct teachings and healthy relational practices before fully understanding the extent of errors in previous ways of thinking and relating. The best way to help a person who has recently left a cult or a controlling religious group is to be a trustworthy friend and let the person process truth about that previous experience at that person's own pace. The deep friendships formed over the years may cause the person to swing from sadness and anger at the lost time spent in the group to justifying the actions of the group and longing to return. In time, the person will be able to see the experience as both positive and negative, for the truth is a blend of the two. Eventually a realization can be reached that meaningful friendships and lasting memories were made in a place that taught or practiced an appealing mixture of truth and error. When the person can release the incorrect teachings and relational dynamics, forgive the teachers or leaders, and yet still cherish the positive aspects of the journey, the spiritual pendulum will return to the center.

The wisdom that waits at the end of a journey through disillusionment is the balance that is restored in a person's life. To bring the pendulum back to center, wrong ways of thinking and behaving must be discarded. However, a person must be careful not to throw away the good from an experience along with the bad. In unhealthy families and churches, questions are discouraged because public impressions become more important than reality and authenticity. Yet questions are vital to the restoration process for a person seeking wholeness. You need to ask yourself what drew you into the group or what kept you from leaving once you began to see the problems. What was the appeal of the false teaching or unhealthy dynamic that led to your disillusioning experience? How will you approach a new church situation in the future? What qualities do you consider important in a healthy leader? Questions help you learn more about yourself, about life and about biblical truth. Questions will keep you from the danger of allowing the pendulum to swing too far to the other side.

To help those going through a period of disillusionment, encourage them to ask themselves the difficult questions so they can face their fears, gain insight and move forward. While the questions may lead to painful answers, ultimately the truth sets a person free (Jn 8:32).

RAINDROPS OF CHANGE

Disillusionment does not always center on a particular relationship, event or error. At times a person becomes disillusioned with flaws in church culture, looking at the system as a whole. That person may become frustrated, assuming this flaw will never be overcome. The tension between the biblical ideal and the current reality is disheartening. Changing the church to conform to the ideal seems too formidable.

The church is God's design, but individual churches and denominations function as human institutions. In such institutions change comes slowly, for institutions are created to maintain stability. Slow change, however, does not mean there will never be change. If you seek inspiration for the possibility of change within church culture, consider the church's view on slavery and race that changed over the course of centuries.

In the twenty-first century, Christians across all denominations recognize that slavery is wrong. A typical churchgoer recoils at the horrors of the transatlantic slave trade that spanned over four and a half centuries, transporting millions of Africans to serve the economic interests of the European colonial powers in the New World. However, individuals today tend to forget that most churches during that time condoned slavery, believing that the Bible provided useful rules to govern the behavior of both the slave and the master. In fact, the largest Protestant denomination in the United States, with over sixteen million members, was founded to defend the practice of slavery. In 1845 during a meeting in Augusta, Georgia, the Southern Baptist Convention became a separate denomination, splitting from northern Baptists over the issue of slavery.

Many masters did not want slaves to learn how to read lest they read in the Bible the teachings of Christ that supported equality. Ignoring Christ's message of racial equality, some ministers instead focused on the passage in Genesis 9:24-27 describing the curse of slavery on the descendants of Noah's son Ham, and there saw justification for en- slaving Africans. The early church from the time of the apostles until A.D. 313 largely ignored the issue of slavery, choosing to focus on the gospel message. The early church recognized that everyone was equal in Christ, with "neither Jew nor Gentile, neither slave nor free, nor . . . male and female, for you are all one in Christ Jesus" (Gal 3:28). The main thrust of the early church was sharing the message of salvation. Trying to bring social change to the Roman Empire at that point in history was not possible for the fledgling church. As a result, the apostle Paul advocated that slaves obey their earthly masters with a sincere heart, recognizing that their reward will come from God (Eph 6:5-8).

From A.D. 313 until the eighteenth century, the church tolerated slavery. Most people were busy leading difficult lives of their own under harsh economic conditions. In the eyes of many people, a slave who was well fed was better off than many poor people who were free. Yet starting in the eighteenth century, a few men and women arose who would turn the tide of history and influence the consciences of their countrymen and fellow churchgoers.

One man who spent his entire lifetime changing attitudes toward slavery was the British politician William Wilberforce (1759–1833). After serving four years in Parliament, Wilberforce became an evangelical

Christian, and his faith changed his outlook on life. John Newton, the author of the hymn "Amazing Grace," provided a strong spiritual influence in Wilberforce's life. In his youth, Newton served as a sailor who participated in the slave trade. Later in life he became an Anglican clergyman and a prominent supporter of the abolition of slavery.

As a young adult Wilberforce joined with his friend William Pitt, who became the youngest prime minister in 1783 at the age of twenty-four, to take on the abolition of the slave trade. Following successful public campaigns that raised awareness of the conditions of slaves, Wilberforce attempted to pass a bill in 1791 abolishing the slave trade, but the bill was defeated by 163 votes to 88. However, Wilberforce continued his work. In March 1796, Wilberforce nearly succeeded in passing a proposal to abolish the slave trade, but the measure was defeated by four votes in the House of Commons. The defeat caused Wilberforce to wrestle with disillusionment. At least a dozen abolitionist members of Parliament missed participating in the vote because they were either out of town or attending the new comic opera in London. He had given his youth and his health to the cause while others did not want to be inconvenienced for the cause.

The war with France distracted Parliament from the issue of the slave trade. In the mind of the general public, abolition became associated with the French Revolution, causing Wilberforce to lose public support. Suffering from a condition thought today to be ulcerative colitis, Wilberforce, now in his late thirties, went to the countryside to rest. He felt discouraged and defeated. He was ready to give up. However, a source of encouragement came into his life. Her name was Barbara Ann Spooner. A month and a half after he met this source of encouragement, Wilberforce married her and renewed his commitment to achieve the abolition of the slave trade.

In January 1806, Wilberforce faced a great loss when his friend William Pitt, the prime minister of England, died. Yet hope was on the horizon in the person of a shrewd maritime lawyer, James Stephen, who suggested taking a new approach to destroying the slave trade. He recommended the introduction of a bill to ban British subjects from aiding or participating in the slave trade to the French colonies. Since the bill prevented British ships from supplying slaves to foreign colonies at war with Britain, the bill appeared to be a patriotic measure more than an abolitionist measure. Wilberforce and other abolitionists remained silent so that no attention was drawn to the real effect of the measure. The bill weakened the British slave trade financially, thus weakening support for the slave trade in Parliament.

In 1807, the new prime minister, Lord Grenville, introduced an abolition bill in the House of Lords, where it passed by a large margin. Finally, on February 23, 1807, as tears streamed down the face of William Wilberforce, a bill to abolish the slave trade was adopted by the House of Commons by 283 votes to 16. As the vote was tallied, members of Parliament spoke in tribute to Wilberforce's efforts across the decades. On July 26, 1833, three days before Wilberforce died, he heard news of government concessions that ensured the adoption of the Slavery Abolition Act, which would outlaw slavery in most parts of the British Empire.[1]

In 1865, the Thirteenth Amendment to the US Constitution passed, outlawing slavery in all the states. In 1995, on the 150th anniversary of its founding, the Southern Baptist Convention voted to adopt a resolution apologizing for its past defense of slavery and renouncing the role that racism played in its early history. In 2012, the Southern Baptist Convention elected its first black president, a New Orleans pastor named Fred Luter Jr.

Change within churches, organizations and society can happen, although often not on the timetable of the person working for change. Many who work for change grow older without seeing their dreams fulfilled. Perhaps, like Wilberforce, their best efforts fail for a season because others are unwilling to make even small sacrifices. Perhaps others misunderstand their efforts, just as some members of Parliament questioned Wilberforce's patriotism. Yet those who do not let disillusionment hinder their continued participation pave the way for future victory. Because he rejected cynicism and allowed no excuses in his life, Wilberforce drew his last breath knowing that his participation changed the world.

Not everyone is called to be a Wilberforce. Some are called to be encouragers, like Barbara Ann Spooner. Others are called to inspire the Wilberforces of the world to action, like John Newton. Yet others provide strategic supporting roles, such as James Stephen. When one raindrop joins with many other raindrops, together they produce a flood of change.

If you are disillusioned with any aspect of the world around you, consider the possibility that you may be called to participate in the solution. For example, if you care about environmental issues, start by providing a recycling bin for your church or urging colleagues in your school or workplace to reduce unnecessary printing of documents. Someday you may influence congregations or corporations to build environmentally friendly sanctuaries, offices or parking lots, but you need to be willing to start small. To fight judgmental attitudes within an organization, become the person who ends conversations that are critical of certain people or groups. Set the standard you wish others would adopt. You may not change everyone, but you will have changed yourself and started a new trend within your circle of influence.

In the process of working for change within any group, recognize your present limitations even as you dream for the future. Do not sow discord within a local church, workplace or other organization while advocating for change. Earn the right to be heard by faithful participation. Work with the leadership. Commit to personal growth and persistence in the face of adversity. In time, you may be able to bring about the needed change in the wider body of Christ or society at large.

As J. R. R. Tolkien wrote in a letter to his son, Michael, "The greater part of truth is always hidden in regions out of the reach of cynicism."[2] Look for the truth hiding behind the illusions. Disillusionment does not need to lead to spiritual stagnation. Your new perspective on reality can become an impetus for growth. Your love for the people who make up the church and community around you can grow even deeper when you are willing to love them as they really are and not as you wish them to be. In return, you might find that they love you right back.

Part Three

RESOLVING DOUBTS

9

An Authentic Journey

This above all—to thine own self be true,
And it must follow, as the night the day,
Thou canst not then be false to any man.

WILLIAM SHAKESPEARE

Then you will know the truth,
and the truth will set you free.

JOHN 8:32

PHYSICAL ACTIVITY CLEARS THE MIND and refreshes the soul. A quick stroll down Commonwealth Avenue in the evening hours transported me to the antidote to long hours in the lab. The gym at the Harvard Club may not have been as extensive as some suburban gyms, but the social aspect made the workout better than any available elsewhere. Interesting people from all walks of life could be found lifting weights after their day of work in the city. You could find an occasional celebrity sneaking in a workout in the privacy the Harvard Club offered.

The fitness facilities, including state-of-the-art squash courts, were located in the basement, surrounding the Grill Bar, which served amazing food capable of undoing any fitness progress made in the gym or aerobics studio. The men's locker room was next to the main fitness desk. A winding staircase next to the squash courts led to the women's locker room, the starting place for my workout experience.

"Hello, Christina, how was your day?" The attendant in the plush woman's locker room greeted each member by name and engaged us in conversation. She stocked fresh towels, took our gym clothes to the laundry and kept the facility sparkling clean. But for each of us, she was so much more than the attendant who made the locker room a peaceful oasis. She was our friend and confidant.

FAITH PERVADING EVERYDAY LIFE

Once the attendant learned I was a Christian, she loved to tell me about her church, her son and the latest sermon she heard. I learned many interesting facts and deep spiritual truths from this Harvard Club employee. One Christmas, I took her to my church when we were having a special service I thought she would enjoy.

She spanned both my university world and my church world with ease. I found her company delightful because she was completely authentic. She would share her spiritual struggles, holding nothing back. She spoke of her failures as readily as her successes. She desired to continue to mature in her Christian walk, but she was comfortable being herself and contributing to all our lives through her job.

The desire to please or impress others can block our ability to be authentic. Fear of offending those who do not share our faith can keep us silent about our beliefs. Jesus said, "Whoever acknowledges me before others, I will also acknowledge before my Father in heaven. But whoever disowns me before others, I will disown before my Father in heaven" (Mt 10:32-33). Faith confined to the private sphere weakens.

Good news, by definition, should be shared. The gospel is spiritual good news worth spreading to everyone we know.

Communicating with others about one's faith should be a natural extension of a Christian's life, and not a duty to check off a list. The communication should be for the benefit of the listener and not the speaker. James wrote to the Jewish Christians,

> What good is it, my brothers and sisters, if someone claims to have faith but has no deeds? Can such faith save them? Suppose a brother or a sister is without clothes and daily food. If one of you says to them, "Go in peace; keep warm and well fed," but does nothing about their physical needs, what good is it? In the same way, faith by itself, if it is not accompanied by action, is dead. (Jas 2:14-17)

Faith can be communicated with words, but it *must* be communicated with actions. The combination of the two delivers the clearest message. Most people are looking not for religious information but for tools to navigate through life. Authentic faith relates to real life like a conversation between two friends. It is at home in the locker room as well as the cathedral.

Advertisement that promises more than a product delivers results in disappointment. People do not want to buy snake oil for their spiritual needs. Better to watch a believer demonstrate faith through the trials of everyday living than to hear persuasive words that sugarcoat the truth. The example of a faith that perseveres through doubts is more powerful than a faith that never questions.

A gospel message that promises becoming a Christian will solve all problems in a person's life sets a new believer up for failure. Making a decision to follow Christ may cause problems for many people in the short run. A new believer may become the target for scorn from old friends. If the person has grown up in a different religious tradition, that person may be disowned by family.

Jesus promised, "I have come that they may have life, and have it to the full" (Jn 10:10). He also said, "Anyone who wants to be first must be the very last, and the servant of all" (Mk 9:35). The truth of the Christian life is a balance between these two Bible verses. Christians live for a purpose greater than their own lives, which helps them experience an abundant life. However, Christians recognize they are no longer the masters of their own lives. At times, compassion for others compels a Christian to become a servant, risking being misunderstood and mistreated.

In describing everyday Christian life to new believers, tell them, "Your faith will teach you how to pray, but you will not be able to pray all future challenges out of your life. While your prayers will give you strength, they will not always give you your way. You will find joy in Christ, but you will walk through spiritual dry spells at some point in your journey. You may even experience periods of great sorrow.

"In the body of Christ, known as the church, you will find a spiritual family. They will carry your burdens and offer you acceptance. But like any family, there will be jealousy, conflict and disappointments. You will need to forgive and be forgiven. You will need God's restoring power many times along the way. You may not have all your expectations granted, but you will have all you need."

FAITH LIVED IN THE MOMENT

Witnessing the reality of death up close through the loss of an immediate family member can change a person's perception of many things in life. Grieving people may enter a time of reflection during which they rethink their choices and their approach to life. For example, I am a cautious person by nature, which I inherited from my mother. I do not walk close to the edge of a cliff or stand first in line at amusement parks. I love the scenery of large, sweeping vistas, but I feel dizzy when climbing to great heights. However, when my father, who enjoyed taking the occasional risk, suggested riding in a hot air balloon together as a remedy for grief after my mother's death, I agreed.

Fresh on my mind was the concept that life can end at any moment. You could die wasting away from cancer, so why not risk the dangers of a ride in a hot air balloon? My father researched the options for this experience and found a place within an hour's drive of my childhood home in Pittsburgh. Balloon rides require still conditions with few breezes, which means the early morning hours right before sunrise provide the perfect conditions. Our balloon-ride package came with a sunrise breakfast to celebrate the experience. In spite of my cautious nature and deep respect for heights, I had no valid reason to say no.

While my logical, cautious self questioned the wisdom of agreeing to ascend to great heights in a small basket, my adventurous side took over the moment we arrived and saw the hot air rushing into the brightly colored balloon. As we rose closer to the clouds and the Pennsylvania farmland stretched out beneath us like the display in a model railroad scene, I felt calm and relaxed. Drifting across the sky, I realized life is too short to ignore adventure. My opportunities to make memories with my mother were over, but I could seize the moment to enjoy the beauty of being alive and share it with my father.

Life is a gift we will miss if we are too careful. Planning for the future, shouldering our responsibilities and working toward goals are prudent actions. However, living authentically also means staying in touch with the present. In the haze of grief that made sustained concentration difficult, the wash of coral sunlight peaking from behind the clouds in the azure sky provided the opportunity to take in the beauty of one hour drifting in the summer breeze with no thoughts for the past or the future. Fully entering the beauty of the moment was a balm for my pain. I felt more alive holding on to the basket than I ever did on the ground.

The houses and cars below looked so small. I understood how trivial our problems must appear to God. Our lives are but a breath. In the towns below, people were waking up to face another day. They were getting dressed, brushing their teeth and trying to find their car keys. Some of them were looking forward to a day filled with celebration. Others were experiencing a time of sorrow, just like me. Many morning prayers were drifting up to heaven, yet God loves everyone enough to give his attention to each petition.

Like time on a mountaintop, time spent in the clouds can last only so long. When we returned to solid ground and headed to the planned breakfast, I felt ready to return to my life with its schedules and intellectual demands. The future waiting for me was a future without my mother, but a future that God had prepared for me nonetheless. My season of grief would change to seasons of celebration. I felt stripped of the protection of one generation standing between death and me. I was now the oldest female in my immediate family. The family traditions now rested with me. I needed to go on.

Jesus understood the value of gaining perspective by pulling away from the crowds for a season of renewal. He also used experiences on mountaintops to instruct and prepare his disciples. Early in his ministry, when he saw the crowds gathering, he went up on a mountainside to deliver his Sermon on the Mount to the disciples who followed him (Mt 5:1). Late in his ministry, he took Peter, James and John up a high mountain to witness his transfiguration and prepare for his coming sacrifice on the cross (Mt 17:1-2).

In our journey of faith, we need times of renewal. These experiences help us make peace with the past and prepare for the future. King David sang of God's compassion shown through his ability to renew our youth like the eagle's (Ps 103:5), enabling us to soar once again. The prophet Isaiah echoed the words of David in this passage:

> Even youths grow tired and weary,
>> and young men stumble and fall;
> but those who hope in the LORD
>> will renew their strength.
> They will soar on wings like eagles;
>> they will run and not grow weary,
>> they will walk and not be faint. (Is 40:30-31)

Renewal is not only for continued strength for the journey but also for fresh consecration. After the prophet Nathan confronted King David regarding his sin with Bathsheba, David wrote these words:

> Create in me a pure heart, O God,
>> and renew a steadfast spirit within me. (Ps 51:10)

An authentic journey of faith will ascend into the clouds and land on the ground, but God is capable of helping us learn to be steadfast throughout it all. His forgiveness can renew us when we need a fresh start. In his mercy, he sees our weakness and reaches down to give us strength once again. He does not quit on us, so we have no excuse to quit on him.

After the sunrise breakfast, the pilot gave us an amusing certificate attesting to our status as balloonists. It was evidence of my momentary bravery and a light note in the day. I brought the certificate back to Boston with me, placing it in the file cabinet in a folder near all my scientific papers. I still have the certificate today, along with the appreciation for the value of a little adventure on the journey of life.

FAITH DEVELOPED OVER TIME

Authentic faith flows freely from a person's real life and encompasses the ups and downs of life. In addition, authentic faith involves growth and development similar to the biological stages of a person's life. Just as each life stage brings unique challenges, each part of our spiritual development comes with distinct tests.

Initially, like young children we might approach our faith with joy and wonder. We learn with delight, pray with great sincerity and grow with relative ease. Of course, in the same way that a small child can become easily distracted, a young believer can wander off on a dangerous path. Learning the truth so we can make wise choices is the test of this season of growth. Peter gave words of advice for this stage of spiritual growth: "Rid yourselves of all malice and all deceit, hypocrisy, envy, and slander of every kind. Like newborn babies, crave pure spiritual milk, so that by it you may grow up in your salvation, now that you have tasted that the Lord is good" (1 Pet 2:1-3).

New believers need to separate from old habits and approaches to life. They need to rid themselves of certain thoughts and behaviors. But being a Christian is not about what you cannot do; it is about who you are and who you have the potential to become. Just as a baby needs nourishment to develop, a young believer needs to learn simple spiritual truths to grow in faith. While the initial decision to become a Christian is important, the process must continue past the initial commitment. A taste of spiritual truth gets us started in the right direction, but we have to keep going.

As we grow as believers, we move beyond our focus on our own growth to concentrate on ministry to others. Like an adolescent forming relationships beyond the immediate family unit in preparation for maturity, tests in this stage of spiritual growth come from the relationships we form with others. Before we can learn to lead others, we first must learn how to follow.

Jesus clearly explained that following means self-denial. "Whoever wants to be my disciple must deny themselves and take up their cross and follow me. For whoever wants to save their life will lose it, but whoever loses their life for me will find it" (Mt 16:24-25). Many times the self-denial does not require a mission trip to a remote area of the world. It just requires getting along with other Christians. Worthwhile accomplishments in ministry usually require teamwork, and teamwork involves self-denial.

How well we work with others will determine our lasting effectiveness. Encounters with others at varying levels of maturity can try our patience and derail our goals. Our ability to lead with integrity opens doors for great effectiveness while our weaknesses can cause others to stumble.

Jesus had harsh words for leaders who caused others to sin by their actions. He said to his disciples, "Things that cause people to stumble are bound to come, but woe to anyone through whom they come. It would be better for them to be thrown into the sea with a millstone tied around their neck than to cause one of these little ones to stumble. So watch yourselves" (Lk 17:1-3).

Authentic faith harbors no illusions about itself. It embraces accountability from others. As we move into maturity, we consider the impact of our actions on the people around us, following the admonition of Paul to the Romans, "We who are strong ought to bear with the failings of the weak and not to please ourselves. Each of us should please our neighbors for their good, to build them up" (Rom 15:1-2).

Though conflict may arise in Christian relationships, the attitude of two believers should always be to meet each other's needs. While such an attitude may not solve all problems, it paves the way to resolution. William Shakespeare offered the following wisdom:

This above all—to thine own self be true,
And it must follow, as the night the day,
Thou canst not then be false to any man. (*Hamlet*, act 1, scene 3)

When we understand our own needs and values, we are ready to present our authentic selves to others. When we know what is important to us in a conflict, we can seek a win-win solution for all sides.

As our faith develops over time, our views and needs will change.

Being authentic requires that we acknowledge those changes while maintaining our core values. Jesus told the Jews who believed in him, "If you hold to my teaching, you are really my disciples. Then you will know the truth, and the truth will set you free" (Jn 8:31-32).

The teachings of Jesus are profound, yet straightforward. He explained the truth about humanity's inability to save itself. He pointed out hypocrisy in religious leaders (Mt 6:5). He showed both the value and the danger of holding on to traditions. He lived life as a simple carpenter but also walked on water (Jn 6:16-21). He observed the Sabbath but valued compassion over legalism, healing a man on the day of rest (Mk 3:1-6). He practiced and preached authenticity. He expects the same of his followers.

While no Christian can live up to the standards set by the Savior, I remind myself that my life may be the first Bible a person reads. If I show a person grace and mercy, I make it easier for him to believe Jesus is willing to offer him grace and mercy. If I listen to her concerns, I open the door for her to listen to the gospel message. When I share of my time and resources to meet someone's needs, I increase the likelihood that this person will believe God wants to meet his or her needs.

When a church offers unconditional love and acceptance to nonbelievers, it is living out the truth in John 3:16 that "God so loved the world." Anyone expecting to find a perfect church or a sinless believer has embarked on a fruitless search. But those searching for authentic faith will be satisfied with a church moving in the direction of Christlike love, exhibiting compassion and meeting the needs of its community. God's power working through human weakness is a testimony worth hearing.

While some people will use the imperfections found in Christians as an excuse to reject the gospel message, the existence of those imperfections and God's remedy for the problem constitute the essence of the gospel message. Honesty and humility can break through people's defenses better than a well-reasoned apologetic defense. When people ask you difficult questions about Christian teachings, your life may be the real answer they are seeking. Realize that you cannot give them more than the story of a pilgrim on an authentic journey, stumbling yet growing, questioning yet believing, and failing but persevering. That story may be all they need to hear.

10

RETRACING THE PATH

*If I had never dropped out, I would have never dropped in
on this calligraphy class, and personal computers might not
have the wonderful typography that they do. Of course
it was impossible to connect the dots looking forward
when I was in college. But it was very, very clear
looking backwards ten years later.*

STEVE JOBS

*Each of you is to take up a stone on his shoulder,
according to the number of the tribes of the Israelites,
to serve as a sign among you. In the future, when your children
ask you, "What do these stones mean?" tell them that the flow of the
Jordan was cut off before the ark of the covenant of the LORD.
When it crossed the Jordan, the waters of the Jordan
were cut off. These stones are to be a memorial
to the people of Israel forever.*

JOSHUA 4:5-7

L ight seeped through the laboratory window, rivaling the brightness from my computer screen. As a connoisseur of sunsets who partook of sunrises only on rare occasions, I was captivated by the opportunity to watch a new day dawn.

Might as well get away from this desk and watch the sunrise. The artistry of the reverse sunset exceeded my expectations, yet the daybreak brought more anxiety than hope. Although the deadline for my thesis defense loomed large, I could not finish my writing without the data from a few critical experiments. My schedule of lab work by day and writing by night worked only for a short sprint, but my race had morphed into a marathon.

When I cross the graduation finish line, I will be done, but not in the way I dreamed all these years. Cancer had claimed my mother and weakened my father while circumstances beyond my control delayed the completion of my research. Time, the fourth dimension in our universe, marched forward one sunrise at a time.

We experience our lives and our journeys of faith along the continuum of time. The future becomes the present, and the present shifts to the past. Many wise words have been written about the importance of moving forward, living in the present and focusing on the future. Yet I wondered if the key to future faith could be found in past milestones. Perhaps I could gain insights useful for my current challenges by retracing the path that led to watching a sunrise from a laboratory window.

Victories from yesterday are easy to forget in the midst of today's struggles. Old questions answered in the due course of time enter the musty archives of unimportance. Memories of God's past faithfulness sit on a trophy shelf in a spare room. Doubts creep into your heart, and you lose courage. What can the past teach the future?

Steve Jobs, the cofounder of Apple Inc., believed reflecting on the past helps you connect the dots to see how certain events prepared you for your most important accomplishments. In his commencement address at Stanford University in 2005, he noted how a calligraphy class he audited after he dropped out of college influenced his creation of a wide range of fonts for personal computers. At the time he took the class he had no idea his casual choice would serve as vital preparation for the future. Retracing the path of your life can reveal how time has transformed pain into purpose and loose ends into an intricate tapestry. The dots of past events often connect to form patterns, swirls of wise and regrettable choices across life's landscape offering perspective for present-day decisions.

THE SOUND OF THE WAVES

Biblical stories indicate that God places value in remembering key moments from the past. In the book of Joshua (Josh 3), the children of Israel are preparing to enter the Promised Land after forty years of wandering under the harsh desert sun in the Sinai Peninsula. Moses, who led them out of slavery in Egypt, is dead, along with all the other men of military age who crossed the Red Sea during the exodus from Egypt. Moses' assistant, Joshua son of Nun, is now in charge of the coming battle to take possession of the Promised Land. Before the children of Israel can fight for their inheritance, they must cross the Jordan River, which separates the wilderness from the Promised Land. At this time of year, the river flows at flood stage, making the crossing difficult and dangerous.

After three days camping near the river, Joshua instructs the priests who will carry the ark of the covenant, "Pass on ahead of the people" (Josh 3:6). Spiritual leadership requires stepping into uncertain waters while others gather their courage on the riverbanks. The priests will be the first to march down the slope to the rushing river. As they step closer to the water, they remember childhood stories of the parting of the Red Sea under the leadership of Moses. How comforting to see Moses standing on the riverbank with an outstretched staff! But

Moses is a memory. Only Joshua, his former servant, is present. Joshua has told them God will do amazing things today. One more step and the priests will know whether Joshua has truly heard from God.

The instant the priests step into the river, they hear the sound of the waves. With a whoosh, the water begins to pile up a great distance away near another town. No water flows at the crossing point. Seeing only firm ground at their feet, the priests carry the ark of the covenant into the center of the river. Here they will wait until everyone else crosses safely to the other side.

This demonstration of God's faithfulness provides much more than convenient transportation across a flooded river. The memory of the miracle will strengthen the faith of the children of Israel as they fight to take possession of the Promised Land. Once the people settle in their houses to begin their new lives, the memory will reinforce the importance of following God's commandments in their new homeland. Crossing a river at flood stage on dry ground is a dramatic event. Yet even dramatic events can be forgotten all too soon in the midst of handling the next crisis. For this reason, God instructed Joshua to have one person from each tribe of Israel pick up a stone from the middle of the river where the priests stood holding the ark of the covenant (Josh 4). Long after the roar of the waters' receding had faded, these stones would stand as a memorial in the Promised Land on the other side of the Jordan River, helping the people remember God's faithfulness and serving as a concrete teaching aide to parents passing their faith to the next generation.

Not every event in life is worthy of collecting memorial stones, but certain moments provide a key to unlock future faith. The twelve stones from the middle of the Jordan River were not the first memorial stones in the Old Testament. The patriarch of the children of Israel, before he bore either the name of the nation or his first offspring, set up a memorial stone that became a lifelong reminder of

God's protection. In Genesis 28:1-22, Jacob, who would be renamed Israel after receiving his degree from the school of perseverance, travels from his home to Paddan Aram, the land of his mother's brother Laban, to find a wife. Weary from traveling, he finds a stone to use for a pillow and drifts into the deep sleep known best by men who labor outdoors. In his sleep, he sees a stairway to heaven with angels ascending and descending and the Lord standing at the top. God reassures Jacob, "I am with you and will watch over you wherever you go, and I will bring you back to this land. I will not leave you until I have done what I have promised you" (Gen 28:15). Early the next morning, Jacob takes the stone he used for a pillow the night before and turns it on its side so it becomes a pillar. Jacob pours oil on the stone to consecrate it and calls the place Bethel, meaning house of God. He vows that if God takes care of him on his journey and brings him safely back to his father's house, then the Lord will be his God, this stone pillar will be God's house, and Jacob will give back a tenth of all the Lord gives him.

Years pass and Jacob acquires two wives, both daughters of his mother's brother Laban. His two wives' handmaidens also become his wives. These four women bear him twelve sons. Jacob acquires wealth and large flocks of livestock. In the midst of his great success in the land of Paddan Aram, which Jacob experiences despite the trickery of his father-in-law, God speaks to him in a dream telling him, "I am the God of Bethel, where you anointed a pillar and where you made a vow to me. Now leave this land at once and go back to your native land" (Gen 31:13).

Jacob had fled his native land because his older twin brother, Esau, wanted to kill him, a valid reason to avoid returning home. Esau felt Jacob had cheated him out of their father Isaac's blessing. In those days, a father's blessing was far more than a few encouraging words. The blessing represented the right to become the head of the family upon the father's death, a conveying of inheritance to the firstborn son. Once a blessing was given it could not be revoked. Now twenty years later, the time had come for Jacob to return home and face his brother, Esau. When God asked Jacob to find the courage to return to his native land, he reminded Jacob of the memorial stone at Bethel, a memento of God's earlier promise to look after Jacob.

On the way to meet Esau, Jacob sends his family and his possessions on ahead and spends the night alone wrestling with God until the sun rises. His struggle goes beyond intellectual doubts to a physical wrestling match. Jacob refuses to let go of God until he is blessed. At daybreak, he receives a blessing that comes with a new name and a permanent limp in his walk. Jacob, "he who supplants," is now Israel, "he has struggled with God." Jacob the deceiver becomes Israel the overcomer. The wrestling match has changed his gait and his life (Gen 32:22-32). The battle won at sunrise after a long, challenging night bears fruit later that day when Jacob reconciles with Esau, and no harm comes to Jacob, his family or his possessions.

The God of Bethel has been faithful to Jacob, who came back from a long journey to be near his native land. But Jacob has not completed his journey. He promised to make the stone pillar at Bethel, God's house, if God brought him back safely to his father's house. Instead of going to Bethel, he sets up camp outside the city of Shechem. This place brings trouble to Jacob's family, teaching Jacob that stopping short of the finish line leads to grief.

In Shechem, Jacob's daughter Dinah is raped, her brothers excessively retaliate, and Jacob needs God's protection from the people of Shechem. When God speaks to Jacob, he tells Jacob, "Go up to Bethel and settle there, and build an altar there to God, who appeared to you when you were fleeing from your brother Esau" (Gen 35:1). Once more, when Jacob is faced with an impending change in a time of distress, God reminds him of the long-ago memorial-stone experience at Bethel.

Jacob had promised that the Lord would be his God, but Jacob's household contains idols, proof of a compromised commitment. Jacob is ready to fulfill his vow completely now. No longer will he tolerate an undone job. He tells members of his household to put away all the idols, purify themselves and even change their clothes before they embark on the journey to Bethel.

In an act that symbolically completes Jacob's retracing of the path to Bethel, he sets up a stone pillar and once again anoints it with oil at Bethel. God confirms to him that he indeed will be the one to inherit the spiritual blessings of his father, Isaac, with these words: "A nation and a community of nations will come from you, and kings will be among your descendants. The land I gave to Abraham and Isaac I also give to you, and I will give this land to your descendants after you" (Gen 35:11-12). Through the twists and turns of Jacob's life, God worked to fulfill his goals for an entire nation.

The stories of Joshua and Jacob challenged me to consider the role of memorial stones in reigniting my faith and sense of purpose. Retracing the path from stone to stone could help me connect the dots and see God at work in the events of my life. My educational experience, like the early years of most careers, began with a dream but became long hours of repetitive and tedious tasks. In those early morning hours, I came to realize that achievement requires carrying out your initial decision beyond boredom, challenges and conflict. When generations of Israelites touched the memorial stones, they heard God's faithfulness echoing in the sound of the waves. What stone did I need to touch?

THE TASTE OF CAVIAR

With a mixture of curiosity and trepidation, I picked up the mother-of-pearl spoon and placed little pearls of briny goodness on the miniature buckwheat pancakes called blini. Feasting my eyes on the crystal

wall sconces, etched mirrors and pink Finnish granite of New York
City's Petrossian restaurant, I convinced myself that anything served
here must taste delicious and proceeded to take a bite.

"Pop the caviar on the roof of your mouth." A member of the
editorial staff at *Glamour* magazine instructed me and nine other
winners of the Top 10 College Women award on the proper protocol
for caviar consumption.

"It tastes amazing—clean and nutty with only a hint of the sea," I
said, surprised to find myself enjoying the delicacy. I took in the
moment—the effortless laughter of the other college students, the
opulent surroundings, the flash of the cameras and the feeling that
anything is possible.

Ten years later as I poured skim milk over cereal for a quick
breakfast to separate my long night of work on my doctoral thesis
from the start of a new day, I needed to remember the taste of caviar.
Those soft, shiny orbs were my memorial stones, capable of helping
me find the proper perspective. The English romantic painter John
Constable (1776–1837), who is known for his beautiful landscape
paintings, once remarked, "I never saw an ugly thing in my life: for let
the form of an object be what it may,—light, shade, and perspective
will always make it beautiful."[1] Like an object in Constable's paintings,
this difficult season of my life held beauty. Cereal days lead to caviar
days. Work and sacrifice lead to celebration.

I did not really desire a serving of caviar, which I have never ordered
again since that celebratory June evening shortly after my twenty-first
birthday. What I needed that morning was a memory of accom-
plishment and context for my current challenges at the end of my
doctoral program at Harvard University. I was reaching for a former
self who possessed a quiet but unshakable confidence.

Sometimes retracing your path can help you find patterns that led
to previous success. Athletes understand the importance of looking

for patterns of success worth repeating. By reflecting on what makes for a successful practice session, athletes know how to prepare for the game. They consider the amount of sleep they had the night before, the particular foods they ate, how they warmed up and what was on their minds. I needed to think like an athlete and reflect on the patterns that helped me reach previous goals.

Before I traveled to New York City to receive my leadership award as one of the Top 10 College Women of my graduating year, I worked to finish an undergraduate honors thesis and study for difficult exams at Penn State University. The leadership award, given by Condé Nast, the publisher of *Glamour* magazine, recognizes ten female college students in America for their achievements across three areas: leadership, community and campus service, and academic excellence. The magazine selected the first group of Top 10 College Women in 1957. As the student marshal of my graduating class, winner of numerous scientific research awards and fellowships, and the student selected from 70,000 others by the governor of Pennsylvania to serve on the university's board of trustees, I handled the heavy workload of leadership on the Penn State board, ministry and academic achievement by focusing wholeheartedly on my goal. I learned how to disband negative thoughts and embrace a confident outlook. I chose to view the work intensity necessary to meet my deadlines as an invigorating challenge instead of an obstacle to success. When I needed a short break, I would walk across the beautiful University Park campus to sit by a fountain surrounded by tall trees. Here I could put the academic stress aside for a few moments.

Only a few more weeks and I will be watching a Broadway play in New York City. From white lab coat to high fashion! I laughed to myself and closed my eyes to concentrate on the sound of the water cascading down the metal sculpture in the middle of the fountain. I imagined the mixture of joy and relief I would feel when I arrived in the hotel lobby in New York City, ready to meet celebrities and achievers from all walks of life.

I just better not show up in the lab wearing too much makeup when I return. Not appropriate for a serious scientist. I jumped off the concrete circle surrounding the fountain and began my brisk walk back to the laboratory. *God has been good to me. He has given me a life where anything is possible!*

A life where anything is possible. My spoon rattled as I dropped it into the empty cereal bowl after that long night writing my doctoral thesis in my scientific research lab. I carried the bowl over to the sink in the galley kitchen in my townhouse and thought about what *possible* had become. Maybe *possible* needs to be big enough to embrace both hardships and prosperity. Perhaps *possible* is what happens when you even out the pattern of spiritual highs and lows, faith and doubts, commitment and questioning. When you leave the Jacob part of yourself behind to become Israel, a person unafraid of moving toward your destiny, maybe then you learn the true meaning of *possible*. Perhaps the future held fewer of my fears and more of my dreams than I could imagine.

I was ready to admit I was like a pawn in a game of chess that could only see one square ahead. I did not understand the purpose of events that moved me in a certain direction or blocked me from moving in another. Victory may lie across the board several steps, but I focused on the danger of the knight looming nearby. Only the chess master views the chessboard from the proper perspective, knows the purpose behind each move and sees the entire board clearly from one side to the other. The passage of time could help me gain a measure of perspective. Time can reveal how weaknesses became strengths and trials served as preparation for challenges waiting a few squares further into the game of life. Although my future was unknown, the perspective I gained from reflecting on the past reminded me of the chess master's wisdom and gave me faith to move forward and trust in God's plan.

THE SMELL OF FRESH INK

When you connect the dots in your life, you may be surprised to find many of your past experiences redeemed with the passage of time. Even as I struggled to type the final chapter of my thesis, my first academic book, I recalled the moments in my life that prepared me to write. As an only child, I spent many quiet hours reading and writing short stories and poetry. Near the end of elementary school, I was chosen by my school district to attend a regional summer institute for the arts to hone my creative-writing skills. When my father, who founded his own corporation in the field of transportation and logistics, decided to start a publishing division, I would join him during the summer on trips to the bookbindery. I learned how the number of words related to folds of pages. I was fascinated by the efficiency of the factory and the promising smell of fresh ink. Visiting the factory meant we would be carrying a box of newly bound books back to my father's office. Those books gave us hope for a better future for the readers, our authors and our corporation.

After my thesis defense, I would be carrying my own copies of freshly printed pages to the university bookbindery. I held the dream that the words on those pages would mean a better future for cancer patients, who might benefit someday from my discoveries. In the two weeks before my thesis defense, writing experience from my past carried me through the blur of research, revisions and exhaustion. As Steve Jobs might have said, the dots began to connect.

Retracing the path to the events that brought you to your present moment can take you on a journey into your past pain. No one likes to dredge up painful experiences to relive once more through memories. Like Ebenezer Scrooge from Charles Dickens's *A Christmas*

Carol, who resisted revisiting his past yet learned valuable lessons from the journey, remembering who we once were may help us understand why we have become the persons we are today. In the Christian worldview, God can turn what was meant for evil into good.

You can find one of the best examples of pain serving a higher purpose in the biblical account of the life of Joseph (Gen 37; 39–45). God gave Joseph a dream of becoming a leader when Joseph was an adolescent. In the short term this dream brought Joseph only pain. His brothers resented Joseph because of this dream and sold him into slavery in Egypt. Although he served his Egyptian master loyally, he ended up in prison because of a false accusation by his master's wife. In the prison, Joseph interpreted the dream of Pharaoh's cupbearer, who was serving time with him. Although Pharaoh restored the cupbearer to his job in accordance with Joseph's interpretation of the dream, the cupbearer forgot about Joseph for two years. Circumstances increased the pain in his life and seemingly moved him further from his dream. Yet the dots in Joseph's life were about to connect to the fulfillment of the very dream that appeared to be fading away.

Pharaoh had a dream that none of the wise men in Egypt could interpret. At this point, the cupbearer remembered Joseph. Joseph correctly interpreted Pharaoh's dream and became the second in command in Egypt. The very path that seemed to take Joseph away from the fulfillment of the dream that God gave him brought him to the right place at the right time for the dream to become reality.

Joseph recognized the greater purpose for the pain in his life, forgiving his brothers and comforting them with these words: "And now, do not be distressed and do not be angry with yourselves for selling me here, because it was to save lives that God sent me ahead of you" (Gen 45:5). Joseph's life was part of a greater plan, and the difficult years prepared him and positioned him for leadership for the good of others.

Joseph served faithfully everywhere circumstances placed him. He exercised his gifts of leadership and wisdom in slavery and prison long before he became ruler over Egypt. His attitude during adversity reflected his continued faith in God and belief in the dream God gave him. When we read his story today, his life journey makes sense. However, Joseph trusted God in advance, before the purpose became clear.

In my own journey, I have observed that pain often comes near a fork in the road. At this decision point, a door may close in a painful way in the short term. Joseph was removed from his family and homeland and sold into slavery in a foreign country. In modern times, doors may close through conflict, illness, financial pressure, rejection or lost opportunities. Only with the passage of time do people realize that the closed door served to direct their path to future blessing. The loss had a purpose. Young adults often experience this process when a relationship ends. The relationship may not have been necessarily bad, but had the relationship continued, the course of their lives would have been different. All that came after the end of that relationship would not be. In time, the young adults, who are no longer young, may realize that their geographical location, their present employment and their children exist as they are because the young adult's life was redirected through the ending of that relationship. Several friends of mine who became pastors later in life experienced a loss of their longstanding secular jobs right at the moment when they were considering going to seminary to enter the ministry. Such dramatic career changes certainly are not easy, especially when financial pressures mount.

Difficult experiences not only alter the course of a person's life, but they change the person. Joseph became a better leader because of his difficult journey. I have a greater trust in leaders who have weathered difficult experiences. They tend to be less self-centered and brash. Adversity helps us realize that the world does not revolve around us. We understand the truth that the world will go on without us, yet we deeply value our opportunity to make a difference.

Leaders who have passed through hard times have a deeper connection to their own humanity. They understand human weakness and the need to receive strength from others. As the Bible says,

> Praise be to the God and Father of our Lord Jesus Christ, the Father of compassion and the God of all comfort, who comforts us in all our troubles, so that we can comfort those in any trouble with the comfort we ourselves receive from God. (2 Cor 1:3-4)

Having experienced comfort from God and fellow human beings during a difficult season, a leader better values compassion and understands how to comfort others.

I once overheard someone working in a food-pantry ministry state to another worker that food nearing its expiration date is fine since anyone using the ministry should realize that "beggars can't be choosers." His attitude demonstrated that he did not understand that "us" and "them" do not exist in God's economy. The line between the person needing ministry and the one who ministers is very thin. A person who has gone through a difficult trial knows that anyone can quickly cross over from one side to the other. With this realization comes the ability to identify with others in their sufferings. Our empathy improves when we can genuinely imagine ourselves in the other person's circumstances. We no longer see ourselves as superior in any way to a person in need of ministry. Instead we recognize that we are fellow travelers on the journey of faith with the person we are presently helping. Jesus himself set the precedent for identifying with others in their suffering as he

> poured out his life unto death,
>   and was numbered with the transgressors. (Is 53:12)

Recognizing one's limits and weaknesses leads to increased wisdom. We develop more realistic plans, set more appropriate expectations for others and minister with authenticity. We are more likely to follow the warning in Galatians 5:26, "Let us not become conceited, provoking and envying each other." As a result, we become like the person described in Galatians 6 who is truly spiritual and able to gently restore others. In James 1:2-4 we read, "Consider it pure joy, my brothers and sisters, whenever you face trials of many kinds, because you know that the testing of your faith produces perseverance. Let perseverance finish its work so that you may be mature and complete, not lacking anything." Persevering through the pain of difficult life circumstances matures our faith and helps us grow to be more Christlike.

John the apostle, who knew so much about the importance of love, underwent a lifetime of persecution. He was once called a son of thunder (Mk 3:17), but John became the disciple that Jesus entrusted with the care of his mother as he was dying on the cross (Jn 19:25-27). In one of John's letters, he demonstrated how to show love with these words: "Dear children, let us not love with words or speech but with actions and in truth" (1 Jn 3:18). In the early church the son of thunder became a calm, wise leader whose deep faith was an example for all.

When you need to make sense of experiences in your life in order to move beyond your doubts, consider the dimension that clocks measure. Time may give you the answers you seek if you are willing to be patient. Memorial stones can help you persevere beyond what you thought was your quitting point. Let the God of Bethel rekindle your faith and restore your courage. Remember the sound of the waves, the taste of caviar and the smell of fresh ink. God is faithful. Success can return. No experience is wasted. Revisit the past so you can choose a better future.

11

THINKING IN COMMUNITY

*The hardest problems of pure and applied science
can only be solved by the open collaboration
of the world-wide scientific community.*

KENNETH G. WILSON

*As iron sharpens iron,
so one person sharpens another.*

PROVERBS 27:17

"A TREE BELONGS ON THE LEFT SIDE OF THE BUILDING."
"Let me put the cross on top of the steeple." "I am going to make the
double doors in the front." The hands of nearly twenty fourth and
fifth graders danced around a church made of pennies standing on a
plywood platform in the center of a long table. Bits of artificial leaves
and stems, pots of paint, and little plastic connectors dotted the pe-
riphery of the church. I stood to the side of the table holding paper
towels at the ready, pleased to see the children engaged in the project
while my husband popped open another pot of paint.

This Sunday school class was a pleasant break in the long workweek in my final year of graduate school. When I connected with my new church, I looked for ways to match my youth-ministry experience to the current needs of this vibrant congregation. The senior pastor suggested we teach a combined fourth- and fifth-grade class. One of the fifth graders was his eldest daughter, so we considered the suggestion a compliment. Although these students were younger than the ones in our youth group, we found they asked many great questions and challenged us to find creative approaches to ministry. By integrating art projects and occasional physical activities with the supplied curriculum, we learned to hold the attention of a class rapidly outgrowing the limited classroom seating space in a church that would soon embark on a building program.

Most of our art projects involved a quick craft that correlated with the main theme of the lesson, such as a refrigerator magnet with the Bible verse for the week or an origami sculpture capable of serving as an object lesson. One project, however, lasted for many weeks and culminated in a presentation of the artwork from the class to the church during a Sunday evening service.

I wanted to find a concrete way for our class to understand the importance of community in the success of a church building project. I found my answer in a novel toy that made it possible to construct model buildings out of pennies using little plastic connectors that held the coins together. To simulate fundraising, the students donated pennies to the project over several weeks. Once we collected enough pennies in a large jar, we were ready to build a church out of the coins.

To give our church a firm foundation, we started with a large piece of plywood and supplies from a model-railroad store. The students painted the plywood and glued grass, bushes, flowers and trees onto the board to create the landscaping around the church. Next, groups of students connected coins to create the walls, windows, doors, roof and steeple for the church. Finally, the students connected the different sections of the church and added a cross on top of the steeple. The project demonstrated the need to contribute resources and work together as a community in order to construct a new church building to expand our outreach. As the coin church neared completion, so did my time as a graduate student at Harvard University. Like a building project or a scientific collaboration, the whole process of questioning your doubts works best when you think through your challenges in community.

JOINING THE COMPANY OF SCHOLARS

The final major barrier between a doctoral student and the graduation ceremony is the thesis defense. At Harvard Medical School, the thesis defense starts with a research talk open to the general public and ends with a question-and-answer session with the faculty on a student's thesis committee. By the time doctoral students reach this stage, they have become the world's experts on their own areas of research. For well-prepared students, the event is more a chance to share their discoveries with other interested faculty members than a test to pass. For me, the event afforded an opportunity to build a bridge between the scientific community and my faith community. I invited a few of my church friends and the senior pastor to my public research presentation. When I saw the pastor taking notes halfway through my presentation, I suspected a sermon illustration in the making. To his credit, the next Sunday morning he integrated into his sermon the description of a cell-cycle pathway relevant to cancer treatment without forcing the spiritual illustration or misinterpreting the scientific data. During that service, parishioners saw a demonstration of the compatibility of faith and science within our church. Neither the pastor nor the scientist worked out all the answers to every theological question concerning science. However, the congregation learned that science was welcome in the pulpit, and faith could thrive in the laboratory.

A bound thesis ready for the archives served as my ticket to the next Harvard commencement ceremony, an event worthy of becoming a memorial stone in the life of each graduate. The pageantry of a Harvard University graduation ceremony is unequaled among American universities. The experience of the large outdoor ceremony underneath the canopy of honey locusts, maples and elms in Tercentenary Theater in the center of Harvard Yard, marked by ancient traditions and formalities, rewards the years of hard work required to earn a Harvard degree. The festivities begin with the cry, "Sheriff, pray give us order!" The Sheriff of Middlesex County, dressed in a top hat, tailcoat and striped pants, arrives riding a white horse. In the seventeenth century, the sheriff's role in the event was less formal and more practical, focused on controlling rowdy students and alumni who indulged in too much celebratory punch and ale. When the sheriff dismounts and pounds his staff three times, decreeing, "This meeting will be in order," the commencement ceremony begins. Students from the Graduate School of Arts and Sciences march into the yard to receive their doctorates dressed in crimson robes trimmed in black velvet embroidered with crow's feet emblems and adorned with black hoods lined in crimson silk. Instead of the typical mortarboard, the doctoral candidates wear a soft, four-cornered, black velvet tam.

Near the end of the ceremony, when the university president confers the degrees for this group, the graduates are welcomed "to the ancient and universal company of scholars," a traditional phrase that accurately describes the life of an academic researcher. The university president admits the seniors of the undergraduate class to "the fellowship of educated men and women." The ceremony concludes with bells ringing from church towers across Cambridge, with at least fourteen churches participating. The jubilant sound marks a milestone in the life of the exiting graduates and celebrates the beginning of the adventures that lie ahead.

The Harvard commencement ceremony recognizes that good scholarship happens in a community. The research of today links with the work of the brilliant minds of the past. This process is in keeping with Proverbs 27:17:

> As iron sharpens iron,
>> so one person sharpens another.

The community of scholars refines and corrects the thinking of any one researcher. Unlike the typical Hollywood portrayal of the lone, mad scientist, scientists rely heavily on one another. The scientific community provides peer review through conferences, publications and grant applications. Scientists share ideas and exchange laboratory materials with each other. Teams of researchers collaborate to solve difficult problems, respecting the unique expertise that each person contributes to the overall effort.

The process of discovery rarely happens in isolation. By asking questions of other scholars and learning from each other, researchers advance knowledge. In many ways, the scientific community offers a good model for those embarking on a journey of faith. Just as a researcher spends solitary moments conducting an experiment or reading scientific literature, a Christian needs to find quiet time to pray and read the Bible. Solitude has a place in both pursuits, but only for a season. A scientist sharpens his insights and connects his work with the discoveries of others by attending both small laboratory meetings and large conferences. A Christian experiences spiritual growth by getting to a know a few people very well in a small group and celebrating with many others in a larger weekly worship service.

In weekly laboratory meetings, a researcher presents raw data to peers for immediate feedback, suggestions and even encouragement. The presenter walks away from the meeting understanding how to perfect a certain laboratory technique and better design the next experiment. The input from others increases the researcher's confidence when facing tough decisions about which lines of experimentation to pursue and which to abandon. The following week, the researcher will have the opportunity to provide the same help to one of his peers. This collaborative process benefits the overall research program of the laboratory as well as the individual researchers.

The head of the laboratory may offer insights during a weekly meeting and make a few announcements related to practical lab matters, but peer interactions remain the focus of the meeting. The meetings usually last one to two hours, and researchers who are not presenting data on a given week bring food to share with the group. My signature contribution was homemade chocolate-covered strawberries, although some weeks I would show up with a less ambitious culinary choice.

Several times a year, a researcher might participate in conferences where a large number of scientists gather and the interactions relate to a particular academic discipline with prominent scientists delivering formal talks from a podium. While such programs usually include question-and-answer sessions after the talks, the ability of the participants to interact with the speakers is limited. However, the transfer of information from the speakers to the audience members is of great value. Researchers in the audience see fresh data not yet published in scientific journals. A keynote address usually integrates the results of multiple scientific papers to provide an overview of a research area, inspiring researchers to expand the frontiers of knowledge.

Just like scientific researchers, Christians need to connect with one another in a variety of settings. Large Sunday morning services offer the opportunity to hear spiritual truth and to worship in unity, while small groups and ministry teams afford opportunities for collaboration. Within a small group, a person can share thoughts on a passage from the Bible or a book the group is studying together. Another member of the group can affirm, expand or refine those thoughts.

When a person feels confused or overwhelmed by life circumstances, other members of the group can offer encouragement and prayer. The Bible offers an analogy comparing Christians in a local church, referred to as the body of Christ, to the human body (1 Cor 12:12-27). Just as the human body is made up of many parts, each with different functions necessary for the overall health of the body, people with different skills, resources and perspectives compose the local church. In the human body, some parts are hidden from view, but their contributions are vital. In the body of Christ, mutual respect produces spiritual growth and effective ministries. There are no unimportant people in a local church. "Now you are the body of Christ, and each one of you is a part of it" (1 Cor 12:27).

Working in a research lab, I quickly came to appreciate the person who washed and prepared the glassware. If we ran out of clean graduated cylinders, beakers and flasks, all the experiments for the day would need to be put on hold. Furthermore, we had to place our trust in the person who prepared the glassware. Any soap residue left behind could ruin an experiment. If the flasks were not sterilized properly, our results would be skewed. Betty, the lady who prepared our glassware, was a member of our research team, and her work was no less important than ours. My scientific adviser taught us to respect all team members by inviting everyone to laboratory social events.

Within my church, I participated in, and eventually led, several different small groups and classes. I also preached in the large Sunday worship services on occasion. As I was studying for my ordination, I would join a group of pastors and seminary students for a prayer meeting on Wednesday mornings. The senior pastor of my church served as an unofficial mentor to me during these years of ministerial preparation. I learned many practical aspects of ministry from him, such as how to prepare sermon notes, put newcomers in a class at ease and deal with administrative details for church events.

Even more important than these skills were the intangible lessons absorbed while in his presence. He knew how to strike the right balance between friendliness and guidance when leading people through troubled waters or navigating interpersonal conflict. He set wise boundaries but extended compassion. He planned thoroughly but made decisions with his heart. Through his efforts, I integrated into a community of faith, first in my local church, then in ever-widening circles throughout the region, the nation and the world.

In the laboratory or in the church, the virtue of humility helps us appreciate the unique contributions each person makes. "Do nothing out of selfish ambition or vain conceit. Rather, in humility value others above yourselves" (Phil 2:3). Humility purifies our motives, helping us look beyond ourselves to the needs of others. We learn to share the credit with others on the team and acknowledge their perspective. Humility produces a realistic view of life, showing us that our role within a given organization is vital but time limited. Once we understand we must someday yield our role to another, we become motivated to teach and train our replacements. We honor one another (Rom 12:10). We experience the freedom to learn from others, recognizing that everyone has something to teach us. We feel less pressure to pretend to be someone we are not. Free to be ourselves, we have more emotional energy to invest in others. In the body of Christ, "if one part suffers, every part suffers with it; if one part is honored, every part rejoices with it" (1 Cor 12:26). When our focus shifts away from ourselves, we can empathize with the burdens of others. When we see another suffer, we are reminded of our own vulnerabilities. To alleviate the suffering of another, we join in the suffering by making sacrifices of our time and resources. Without the distractions of envy and jealousy, we experience freedom to celebrate the successes of others. God's blessings in their lives remind us of God's faithfulness in our own, and we rejoice.

Like the recent Harvard graduates who join the ancient and universal company of scholars, a Christian joins not only a local group of believers but also the Christian community throughout the ages and throughout the world. After Hebrews 11 lists the heroes of faith whose stories are preserved in the Old Testament, Hebrews 12:1 offers this admonition: "Therefore, since we are surrounded by such a great cloud of witnesses, let us throw off everything that hinders and the sin that so easily entangles. And let us run with perseverance the race marked out for us." The great cloud of witnesses is the ancient company of believers whose wisdom and example serve to inspire us today.

Following Faraday

In academic circles, researchers value history. The Center for the History of Medicine at the Francis A. Countway Library of Medicine located at Harvard Medical School holds more than 212,000 volumes of rare books and special collections spanning more than eight hundred years. The voices of medical scholars through the ages speak to us today through these books, teaching us lessons about the practice of medicine and the interplay between science and society.

As we enter an era when scientists need less than two weeks' time to decipher a person's entire genetic code from a drop of blood or saliva, the work of a nineteenth-century monk growing thousands of common pea plants for eight years in a quiet monastery garden in Austria remains relevant. While the work of Gregor Mendel (1822–1884) was not adequately appreciated until two botanists rediscovered it sixteen years after his death, today we recognize his work as foundational to the study of genetics. Before Oswald T. Avery discovered in 1943 that DNA carries genetic information and before Francis Crick and James Watson determined the structure of DNA in 1953, Mendel concluded that discrete "units" or "factors," now called genes, passed from one generation to the next determine inheritance of traits.

In an era when leading researchers concentrated on phenotype, the outward display of traits, Mendel pioneered the concept of genotype, the genetic blueprint.

Mendel also recognized that an individual inherits one gene from each parent for a given trait, and sometimes an individual may not outwardly display a trait but still be able to pass that trait on to an offspring. Our modern understanding of genetics, although more complicated than Mendel's model, builds on his principles. Study of Mendel's experiments is the starting point for any student of genetics. His careful planning, thoroughness and perseverance demonstrate characteristics any researcher would do well to emulate.

Christians throughout the ages offer the wisdom of their example to us as well as valuable perspective on the foundational truths of our faith. The apostle Paul's insights on church life apply to churches of all sizes and denominational backgrounds. Through the writings of the early church leaders, we can learn how to develop a disciplined prayer life and become servant leaders. Reading books by great Christian thinkers from previous eras helps us gain a perspective on faith beyond the narrow confines of our own time and culture. In the life of a nineteenth-century scientist who also served as a preacher within his church, I found someone who was as comfortable in the pulpit as in the laboratory.

Historians of science consider Michael Faraday (1791–1867), a British physicist and chemist, the greatest experimentalist of all time. I first encountered Faraday in my high school physics class when we reached the chapter on electromagnetism. Michael Faraday discovered electromagnetic induction, showing that the electromagnetic effect of a current in one wire could generate electricity in another wire. He also showed how a changing magnetic field induces an electric current in a nearby circuit. These discoveries are the basis of transformers, generators and electric motors. In fact, he invented the first electric motor. His research laid the groundwork for the world we enjoy today when we drive our cars, switch on lights and clean our clothes in a washing machine. In my high school textbook, I knew him as the man who lent his name to the Faraday constant, the amount of electric charge on a mole (6.022169×10^{23}) of electrons. This number, 96,485.3365 C/mol, was first determined using Faraday's first law of electrolysis. His two laws of electrolysis showed the interdependence of electrical and chemical concepts.

He also appeared in my textbooks as the man honored in the naming of the farad, the International System of Units (SI) derived unit for capacitance. I memorized the equations and laws as an undergraduate in college, but I never knew much about the man behind the discoveries until I read the text of a talk given by Dr. Ian H. Hutchison, professor of Nuclear Science and Engineering at Massachusetts Institute of Technology. While in graduate school, I was asked to speak on the topic of the compatibility of faith and science for a gathering of international students interested in learning more about American culture. For one section of my talk, I wanted to give examples of scientists throughout history who integrated their faith with their quest for scientific knowledge. My research led me to Dr. Hutchison's talk, "Michael Faraday: Scientist and Nonconformist."[1] I learned that not only was Michael Faraday a practicing Christian, but he also served for a season of his life as an elder in his local congregation, preaching in the services and providing pastoral care.

Beyond providing me with good material for my upcoming talk, my research on the life of Michael Faraday allowed me to connect with a mentor from the pages of history. Faraday approached both faith and science as a search for truth, respecting both disciplines on their own terms. He founded his scientific knowledge on carefully observed facts and said, "Without experiment I am nothing." In his day, he could check the work of his colleagues by trying to repeat their findings in the laboratory. This practice continues among scientists today, although the expansion of scientific knowledge limits researchers to a narrow area of expertise. Faraday could set up experiments to verify known discoveries across the disciplines of both chemistry and physics, with no need to trust information solely on authority. In addition to his scientific discoveries, Faraday invented laboratory equipment still used by researchers today, such as the Bunsen burner and test tube. His development of these tools speaks to his commitment to experiments as the key to verifying scientific theories.

In the same way that Faraday verified scientific theories through experimentation, he verified spiritual experiences and religious teachings by reading the Bible. He said, "The Christian who is taught of God . . . finds his guide in the Word of God . . . and looks for no assurance beyond what the Word can give him."[2] The Scriptures were his spiritual foundation just as experiments were his scientific foundation.

Knowledge that a scientist of Faraday's stature prepared sermons as well as university lectures validated my own journey. From my freshman year in college to my final year of graduate school, I accepted offers to speak in churches across the denominational spectrum. Ministry seemed like a natural outgrowth of my faith. My interest in cancer research grew from my desire to see people healed from a physical disease. Ministry was a means of bringing healing to people on the emotional and spiritual level. Medical research and ministry were part of the same caregiving spectrum for helping people lead healthy and fulfilling lives. I appreciated the value of both professions and did not limit my interest to either one. Like Faraday, I preached in the pulpit on Sunday and conducted experiments in the laboratory the rest of the week.

Halfway through graduate school, I attended an ordination ceremony for the first time. During this event, my heart opened up to the possibility of becoming a minister and training for professional lifelong vocational ministry. Several years later, the call to ministry crystallized in my life when I began to understand the role of ordination in the context of community. Formal entry into the ministry represented so much more than the choice of a profession. Becoming a minister meant presenting the personal experience of sensing God's call on my life to a community of ministers for confirmation. Recognition of that call would mean accepting accountability, committing to ministerial development and gaining an opportunity to influence others. Just as peer review protects the integrity of scientific research, belonging to a fellowship of other ministers upholds the integrity of Christian service. When I traveled to speak in churches throughout my denomination, I would enter the pulpit with the same training and credentials as the local pastor who typically preached to that congregation.

No church, denomination or ministerial fellowship is perfect. However, when we choose to participate in a given community, we gain the opportunity to shape that community even as we are shaped by it. While one person can make a difference, that difference happens from the influence one has on the many. By joining a cooperative fellowship of ministers, I would become a bridge between the scientific community and the faith community, following Faraday in the pulpit as well as the laboratory.

RECEIVING A MANTLE AND A CLOCK

In my denomination, the Assemblies of God, the ordination ceremony takes place at the yearly regional ministers' meeting. Ministers from Massachusetts, Connecticut and Rhode Island gather in a special evening service after the district business meetings during the day. While church members can travel to the meeting site to attend the service, I think the choice of a ministers' meeting for an ordination ceremony is fitting. The setting allows current ministers to affirm the calling of new ministers while also remembering their own commitment to a life of ministry.

Symbolism can be a powerful tool for conveying concepts. The central symbolism of the ordination ceremony honors the continuity of leadership within a community. At the beginning of the service, the presbyters, who represent a geographical area containing many churches, enter the service wearing scarflike mantles around their necks and hanging down the fronts of their suits. Each mantle is crimson on one side and white on the other. The white side contains the denomination's shield and the year of the ordination embroidered in crimson thread. The presbyters enter wearing the ordinands' mantles with the crimson side facing up, followed by the ordinands wearing no mantles. At the appropriate moment in the service, one presbyter stands before each ordinand, and the presbyter takes the mantle, flips it over to the side with the shield and year of ordination, and places the mantle on the ordinand.

The transfer of the mantle from the presbyter to the ordinand recalls the biblical story of the transfer of leadership between the prophets Elijah and Elisha (2 Kings 2:7-15). When the established prophet Elijah was taken up to heaven in a whirlwind, his cloak (or mantle) fell to Elisha, who became the next leader of the prophets in Elijah's place. While the new ordinand does not take the place of the presbyter in the same way that Elisha immediately stepped into the role of Elijah, the transfer of the mantle represents the passing of God's anointing, or calling, from one generation to the next.

At the end of the Harvard graduation ceremony, I joined the company of scholars. At the conclusion of the ordination ceremony, I belonged to a fellowship of ministers. In both cases, I recognized the importance of community, acknowledged the end of one journey and prepared to embark on new adventures.

By the time of my ordination ceremony, my church was in the

midst of a building program. We were meeting in the cafeteria of the Christian Book Distributors building while the old church sanctuary underwent reconstruction. During a Sunday morning service at this location, the church presented me with two gifts, a check and a desk clock with two pen stands attached. I remember accepting these gifts while holding my firstborn daughter, then a toddler, on my hip. One of the gifts sits on my desk today. The gift captured both my scientific and my ministerial identities inscribed on a small name plaque on the stand. At the time I received the gift, the plaque symbolized the completion of my educational journey in both ministry and science. I had crossed both finish lines, receiving my PhD in virology from Harvard University in 1999 and my ordination as an Assemblies of God minister in 2004. My dreams had been too small. I learned my family was larger and my community was broader than I had ever imagined.

The clock on my desk has kept time for me in the years since my ordination. Its presence helps me finish assignments on time and know when to push away from my desk to prepare a cup of tea. The clock also reminds me that faithfulness over time is the true way to establish the validity of a calling. Disappointments, doubts and distractions occur in life, but an authentic calling will withstand all challenges.

I have reached for the pens in the stand, one in black ink and the other in blue, many times to jot down a quick note, sign a check or finalize an agreement. The pens recall the importance of keeping commitments in fulfilling a calling. I have learned that my integrity as a Christian leader rests on honoring my commitments to tasks. Do not make promises unless you are able to deliver. Finish what you start. Do your best each time. A Christian leader also must keep commitments to people. We must be willing to love people through difficult seasons, through times of opposition and during their unlovable moments. Not everyone within a community will see things our way, yet we should endeavor to maintain our commitment to the greater vision.

Ultimately, God is the one who provides the strength to keep commitments. As Paul explains in Philippians 1:6, "he who began a good work in you will carry it on to completion."

If you want to build a bridge, you must be willing to keep building one piece at a time. Yet bridge building is not a job you do alone. You need the help of a community in which people rely on each other, learn from each other and build on one another's successes. Both the scientific and the Christian communities include the company of scholars and the cloud of witnesses who have gone before us. Like Elisha who asked for a double portion of the blessing that had been bestowed on his mentor Elijah's life, each generation should seek to have a greater impact than the previous one. Just as current scientists find solutions to problems once thought unsolvable, Christians must love deeper, reach further and communicate clearer than ever before.

When you need to question your doubts, do not face that challenge alone. Seek answers in community. Find a mentor who has walked through similar challenges and kept his faith alive. Find a friend to walk alongside you and share your struggles. Read the Bible, and find a hero of the faith to serve as an example. Reach back in history to learn wisdom from previous generations who once asked the same questions.

If you are seeking a church, look for a place where you feel welcomed, where your own spiritual needs are met, and where you are able to use your gifts and abilities to build up others within the community. Make sure the church emphasizes biblical truth over human personalities and practices collaboration in place of competition. Be prepared to offer grace to others, realizing no community is perfect.

While not everyone is called into the vocational ministry, every Christian is called to a role of service within the local church. Mentoring within the church is a means for transferring the mantle from someone experienced in a role to someone interested in learning the role. The church is more than the current group of people worshiping together on a Sunday morning. The church stretches into the past and looks to the future. One generation receives the mantle and then must pass it along to the next. In the blink of an eye, students grow up to become the next generation of teachers.

12

An Incomplete Process

*In the long run, we shape our lives,
and we shape ourselves. The process never ends
until we die. And the choices we make are
ultimately our own responsibility.*

Eleanor Roosevelt

*For this very reason,
make every effort to add to your faith goodness;
and to goodness, knowledge; and to knowledge, self-control;
and to self-control, perseverance; and to perseverance, godliness;
and to godliness, mutual affection; and to mutual affection, love.
For if you possess these qualities in increasing measure,
they will keep you from being ineffective and
unproductive in your knowledge of
our Lord Jesus Christ.*

2 Peter 1:5-8

GENTLE RAIN FELL AS I PULLED MY SUITCASE past Union Square to Powell Street. I had an airplane to Boston to catch that November morning, but I did not want to leave San Francisco without riding on the iconic Hyde and Powell Street cable cars. As my suitcase thumped along the sidewalk, my fun-loving self debated with my practical self.

"Who knows when you will have another opportunity to return to the city?"

"You'd better be able to find a taxi to the airport at the end of the cable car line or you will miss that long flight back to Boston."

"What a perfect San Francisco day! A light rain, pleasant temperature and slight fog. Ride the car—you won't regret it!"

I rode the car.

In a shining example of God's grace and favor on my trip, a lone taxi was waiting for me at the end of the line just before Ghirardelli Square. The friendly taxi driver served as an impromptu tour guide as we drove down the highway along the bay. He also got me to the airport in time to eat a late breakfast and rest a few minutes before boarding the plane.

A little toy cable car and a cable car Christmas ornament were packed in my return suitcase for my two daughters. Most of the time, the girls traveled with me when I spoke, but this trip to the opposite coast I made alone. Seven and a half years after my ordination, I still enjoyed bridging the worlds of science and ministry. My formal education was long behind me, but the process of learning continued, for the more I learned, the more I realized how much I did not know. Answering questions from audiences after talks challenged me to keep pace with new scientific discoveries and reminded me that education is an ongoing task.

CABLE CARS AND CONNECTIONS

Relaxing in my seat by the window as we prepared for takeoff, I felt relieved that I had made all the right connections from cable car to taxi to airplane. I reflected on how this trip to San Francisco was all about connections—connections in my life as well as my modes of transportation.

I was invited by the American Association for the Advancement of Science to give a talk at the annual joint meeting of the Society for Biblical Literature and the American Academy of Religion on the topic of integrating science into seminary training. I would have never imagined having such an opportunity to build a bridge between science and faith as a graduate student. I also would not have imagined that the president of Harvard University would be a woman (Drew Gilpin Faust) and the head of the National Institutes of Health (NIH) would be an outspoken Christian (Francis Collins) who wrote a book about faith and science.[1] In the twelve years since I had defended my thesis, the world had changed in many ways, including an increased openness to spirituality among scientists and to science among ministers.

Beyond the chance to explore San Francisco, the trip provided the opportunity to reconnect with Kelly Monroe Kullberg, who started the Veritas Forum on the Harvard University campus in my early years of graduate school. I also heard a wonderful talk by Jennifer Wiseman, a Harvard graduate in the field of astronomy who was now the head of the Dialogue on Science, Ethics, and Religion (DoSER) for the AAAS (American Association for the Advancement of Science). The three of us had all passed through Harvard during the same time, leaving with a passion for integrating faith and academics.

The opportunity to spend a little time with these women felt like the continuation of a process started in graduate school and the beginning of new opportunities for the future. The journey of faith is like a friendship that spans the years. A friendship may take on one purpose in a certain season of life and a different one years later. Billy Graham once said, "Being a Christian is more than just an instantaneous conversion—it is a daily process whereby you grow to be more and more like Christ."[2] Just as friendships develop over time, our faith grows stronger through an ongoing process.

The process of questioning your doubts and growing in faith will last a lifetime. Knowing that no Christian achieves perfection in a human lifetime can encourage a person to accept challenges to faith without surprise or guilt. One challenge may resolve, but a new one may take its place at a later time. King Hezekiah became king of Judah when he was twenty-five years old. Soon after assuming power, he fixed the mistakes of his father, King Ahaz. He got rid of the idols and altars to the idols throughout his kingdom. However, he would face different challenges later in his reign, most of his own making.

Hezekiah followed the Lord and enjoyed success in the early years of his reign (2 Kings 18:1-8). However, new challenges arose in the fourteenth year of his reign (2 Kings 18:13–19:37). Sennacherib king of Assyria attacked and captured all the fortified cities of Judah. In response, King Hezekiah stripped the gold from the doors and doorposts of the temple of the Lord and took all the silver in the temple and in the treasuries of the royal palace and gave all of it to Sennacherib to appease him.

However, Sennacherib sent a field commander to demoralize King Hezekiah's subjects and persuade them to surrender to Sennacherib. King Hezekiah needed to decide what to do. He had put God first as a young twenty-something king and experienced great success. Now, although he looked to the Lord, this foreign ruler was waiting to attack at the gates. He had no more silver or gold to give away. He could either fight with the risk of great loss or surrender. Neither choice was appealing.

Fortunately, Hezekiah made the right choice when he decided to seek wisdom from God before taking any action. He consulted with the prophet Isaiah, who told him that God had a third choice that involved neither fighting nor surrendering. God would allow Sennacherib to hear a certain report that would make him return to his own country where he would be killed by the sword. In essence, God would take care of the situation for Hezekiah.

After the word from the prophet, Hezekiah received a letter from Sennacherib saying, "Don't let the god you depend on deceive you by saying he will deliver you. None of the gods of the other nations that were destroyed by my forefathers delivered them" (2 Kings 19:10-11 paraphrase). Hezekiah could give in to his doubts about God's deliverance or trust the word of Isaiah. He took the letter from Sennacherib and spread it out in the temple. Then he began to pray. In his prayer, he acknowledged the historical truth of the destruction of other nations by the Assyrian kings. Hezekiah faced reality. However, Hezekiah's faith superseded that reality, and he began to pray for God's deliverance.

When Hezekiah was a young king, he needed the courage to bring spiritual reform to his own nation. Fourteen years later, he needed the courage to face an external enemy. The test of his faith was not a one-time experience but an ongoing process.

Even as I marveled at the opportunity to combine ministry and science at the conference in San Francisco, the challenges in integrating these fields remain. Not all scientists welcome a dialogue with religion, and many ministers become suspicious of anything related to science. In trying to build a bridge between these two camps, I have learned to be careful not to fall into the water.

However, I remain confident that the key to a greater understanding between scientists and ministers will come from making connections. If pastors reach out to scientists within their congregations to learn more about their work, then science might not feel so intimidating.[3] If scientists share how they integrate their faith and their profession with seminary students, then the next generation of pastors will be better equipped to minister to those with technological backgrounds.[4] The friendships that form between individual scientists and individual ministers will become the bridge between the two professions. With mutual respect in place, dialogue becomes much easier.

LINES AND CIRCLES

Time moves in a linear direction, but we tell time based on cyclical natural processes. We mark a day based on the earth's rotation on its axis, a month based on the orbit of the moon around the earth and a year based on the orbit of the earth around sun. Thus, while time moves forward, the natural processes we use to measure time come back around.

Our spiritual growth process mimics the linear and cyclical processes found in creation. Psalm 1:3 likens a righteous person to

a tree planted by streams of water,
    which yields its fruit in season
and whose leaf does not wither—
    whatever they do prospers.

The growth of a tree is upward and outward, a linear pattern of increasing strength and fruitfulness.

At other times, our spiritual growth resembles the story line from the book of Judges where God delivers his people only to have them turn from him once again. When the consequences of their spiritual decline build up to a certain level, they cry out for the Lord's deliverance. He delivers them, and the cycle repeats again (Judg 10:6-8). You wonder why they never learned from their past experiences. You keep hoping you will turn to the next page and find they finally got it right.

In our spiritual journey, we move forward and also come back around. We grow in our knowledge, our strength and our persistence. We are like the tree planted by the streams of water. We move forward. Then we experience new situations that bear a resemblance to old ones we faced. While we cannot make choices that alter the past, these second chances give us the opportunity to demonstrate to ourselves that we learned the old lesson. Sometimes we fail like the children of Israel in the book of Judges. Life has come back around, and we make a second orbit around the sun. Time has marched forward, but we have circled back to a familiar spot.

Ecclesiastes 1:9-10 delivers this somewhat depressing message:

What has been will be again,
    what has been done will be done again;
    there is nothing new under the sun.
Is there anything of which one can say,
    "Look! This is something new"?
It was here already, long ago;
    it was here before our time.

Such words break the heart of a scientist who hopes to discover something new under the sun. Of course, certain technologies seem new to our generation. Certain discoveries do bring new knowledge and a deeper understanding. However, where faith meets science, we realize human needs stay the same. We once met our need for communication through the use of a quill pen. Now we use computers. In my teen years, I prepared papers for class on a typewriter. How happy I was to prepare my undergraduate honors thesis on a new Mac SE. My doctoral thesis was born on a convenient laptop computer, but one much slower than the laptop I use now.

While I am grateful for the upgrade from a quill pen, my desire to communicate my thoughts is older than parchment paper. There is nothing new under the sun. For this reason, science will bring convenience and a longer lifespan, but certain human needs will continue to fall outside the bounds of technology. We ask the same philosophical questions that the ancient Greeks asked, and new generations will ask the same questions that we ask.

We look to the sky through powerful telescopes and see deeper into the history of the universe revealed through distant stars. Our sophisticated calculations belie a similar search for purpose and perspective shared by nomads staring at the sky while warming themselves around a campfire on a cold desert night. God told Abram, later renamed Abraham, to go outside his tent and look up at the stars in order to understand the magnitude of what God had planned to do in his life. "'Look up at the sky and count the stars—if indeed you can count them.' Then he said to him, 'So shall your offspring be'" (Gen 15:5).

Abraham did not understand modern astronomy, but he saw the vastness of the universe in the desert sky, and he comprehended the omnipotence of the God he served. For a moment, he glanced down the corridors of history to see the kingdoms of the future populated with his descendants. Perhaps there is less poetry in the intricate calculations of light years and dark matter than there is in twinkling stars above a stretch of desert sand, but by measuring the details of our universe we can learn lessons through our telescopes just as important as the ones learned by Abraham with the naked eye.

We see a universe where we are insignificant inhabitants, yet one finely tuned for our existence. These discoveries force a certain humility upon us as we learn that neither the stars nor the sun revolves around us. However, our ideal distance from the sun and the presence of water in liquid form on our planet remind us we are fortunate. You could conclude that the physical constants in the universe in general and in our world in particular hint that this place was prepared for us. Perhaps we are special after all, even if we are not at the center.

Abraham needed to walk many circles in his spiritual life before he experienced the fulfillment of the promise in the birth of his son Isaac. The Bible tells us, "Abram believed the LORD, and he credited it to him as righteousness" (Gen 15:6). However, we see that faith tested many times. Soon after receiving the promise of God, Abram agreed to the

suggestion of his wife, Sarai, to try to conceive an heir with her
Egyptian maidservant, Hagar (Gen 16).

This step is like partial-credit faith. Abram went off the course of
God's plan in an attempt to make God's plan come true through
human effort. People of faith throughout the centuries have repeated
Abram's mistake in their spiritual journeys. Well-meaning attempts at
rushing a dream forward before its time have resulted in conflict and
heartache for many, just as Abram's actions created strife in his family
and between the nations descended from Isaac, born from his wife,
and Ishmael, born from his wife's maidservant, Hagar.

However, the circle came round again, and God met with Abram
when he was ninety-nine years old. God said to him, "I will make my
covenant between me and you and will greatly increase your numbers"
(Gen 17:2). God provided confirmation of his earlier promise to
Abram to strengthen his faith, even after Abram had wandered off
course. God renamed Abram, calling him Abraham, meaning father
of many, and Sarai became Sarah. In changing the names of Abram
and his wife, God confirmed the route through which he intended his
promise to be fulfilled. God said of Sarah, "I will bless her and will
surely give you a son by her. I will bless her so that she will be the
mother of nations; kings of peoples will come from her" (Gen 17:16).

Abraham's response was to laugh and say to himself, "'Will a son be
born to a man a hundred years old? Will Sarah bear a child at the age
of ninety?' And Abraham said to God, 'If only Ishmael might live under
your blessing!'" (Gen 17:17-18). Some promises of God seem too good to
be true, and we greet them with the laughter of disbelief. Like Abraham,
we hope that God will bless our more reasonable plans, instead of
stretching ourselves in faith to trust God for his impossible plans.

God loved Abraham so much that he would not let him settle for
less than God intended him to have. God let Abraham go through
the circles in his spiritual journey in order to prepare him to become

the father of many and an example of faith to generations to come. Sometimes when you feel like you are going around in circles in your spiritual life, consider the possibility that God loves you too much to let you stay the way you are. Maybe your seasons of faith and doubt, which feel like a vicious circle, are also moving you forward in a linear path to the fulfillment of God's promises for your life.

God also loved the nations to come too much to let Abraham settle for less than God intended. If Isaac were never born, he would never have had a son named Jacob, who became Israel. Israel became the father of the nation of God's chosen people. One of the sons of Israel was named Judah. Through the descendants of Judah, God gave King David to the people of Israel. Jesus descended from King David's line. Thus, the birth of Isaac set in motion a lineage that resulted in the birth of the Savior. You could extrapolate from the story of Abraham that God so loved the world that he could not let Abraham settle for less than the best.

Drops and Ripples

The choice you make at any one moment in your life may seem insignificant at the time, like a single drop of water plopping into a pond. You do not see or hear a big splash when the droplet breaks the surface, yet time can amplify the decision like ripples flowing outward in concentric circles from the entry point. The magnitude of these consequences helps us detect the importance of a past event in our lives.

Like the birth of Isaac, one event in your life can have repercussions in the lives of many. Even something as seemingly trivial as teaching a Sunday school class in your church can impact many people in the years to come. Never think small acts of service do not matter in God's kingdom. You cannot judge the future fruit of a choice when you plant a seed.

The night my combined fourth- and fifth-grade Sunday school class presented their coin church to the congregation, a college president delivered the sermon as our guest speaker. Amused by the presentation, he talked with me after the service and learned about my science and ministry background. A year and a half later he invited me to speak at a chapel service on his campus and serve as a guest lecturer for several classes. Eleven years after I spoke in chapel I became a member of the college's board of trustees. During the orientation session for new members of the board, I reminded him of the coin church responsible for connecting us together in ministry more than a decade earlier.

The students in my class grew up, and now many of them fill leadership positions in our church or in one of the three daughter churches planted by our church in nearby towns. During the time I was writing this book, I went to the bridal shower of the pastor's youngest daughter, one of my former students, who was engaged to the youth pastor of our most recent church plant. Standing by the door to greet me was the bride's older sister, another one of my former students, handing out the shower games. As a fifth grader, she was the natural leader of the class, a foreshadowing of her future role leading our youth group alongside her husband. Each summer she organizes the annual mission trip for youth for churches in Massachusetts, Connecticut and Rhode Island, expanding her influence to another generation of youth.

I chose to sit at a round table draped in purple at the far side of the room and watched the other women enter. I was surprised to recognize so many of the young women as the students I taught in my fourth- and fifth-grade Sunday school class years ago. During the course of the event, I had the opportunity to speak with many of them. One young lady, who was kind and mature beyond her years when she was a student in my fifth-grade Sunday school class, told me she had just graduated from nursing school. I have no doubt she will make a compassionate nurse for her fortunate patients. Before the dessert course, I walked up to another student who I remembered had a wonderful sense of humor and a love for horses as an eleven-year-old. What a delight to discover that her wit had sharpened over the years, and now, in her twenties, she rides horses in riding competitions. After fifteen minutes of conversation with her, I realized she had become the kind of person I would choose as a friend. On my way to the room where the bride would open her gifts, I talked with another student who had returned a week earlier from a mission trip to India. Before I left the bridal shower, I met students who taught youth and children's classes, taking the place I had filled many years ago.

More than 1,500 people now stream through the doors of our church each Sunday. Just as one generation grows up and gives birth to another generation, our church has given birth to new churches in the surrounding towns. Each time our church would send an associate pastor along with a core group of fifty or more people from our congregation to establish a new church. The daughter church would benefit from the resources and example of the mother church while developing a unique style appropriate to the new community where the church was planted. The first daughter church planted nearly twelve years ago now serves four hundred people. The other two daughter churches serve approximately one hundred people in each congregation. Together, more than 2,100 people celebrate a vision for outreach that began twenty-five years ago with fifty faithful people and the current senior pastor and his wife.

Like the process of developing new teachers and leaders, the process of planting churches never reaches completion. In fact, our church plans to decrease the interval between launching one church plant and planning for the next one so we can start a new church every two or three years. The impact of church planting amplifies with time. A new church creates more opportunities for people to serve in ministries and grow in their leadership capabilities. Someone who served once a month in the nursery of a large church may now organize the nursery ministry for the church plant. In a church plant, everyone is new to the church, making newcomers fit in more readily than in an established church where a newcomer can feel left out of a circle of long-standing relationships. By the very nature of the start-up process, a church plant spurs creative approaches for engaging with the community beyond the walls of the church.

The best dividends come from investing in people. When you help one person question doubts and move forward in faith, you hear a single drop break the surface of the water. Ripples inevitably follow. The actions flowing from one person restored to spiritual health will impact people within that person's circle of influence. The positive changes within this group will continue to amplify and bless the larger community.

On my way to the parking lot after the bridal shower, I stopped to look up at the church building. Time had changed the configuration of the buildings and the roles of the people who attend, yet the mission and message of the church remained as I found them on my first visit years ago. My ministry has expanded far beyond twenty or so elementary students, but the ripples from my first volunteer assignment continued to flow outward as far as India and as close as a children's ministry attended by my daughters and taught by one of my former students.

I still find science everywhere, much as I did years ago in the glass greenhouses of Phipps Conservatory. I find science when I work within the scientific community on projects in both academia and industry, and I find science through the wonder in the eyes of my two daughters as they learn how the world operates through study and exploration. Ministry and science have found a balance in my life, each enriching my life in a different way.

Your journey will take its own shape, moving you in lines and circles, connecting you to people and places, and providing opportunities for you to have an impact that starts as a drop but becomes a ripple. No human knows what the future will bring. New doubts may rise on the horizon tomorrow, bringing more questions than answers. However, I am confident that there is One wise enough to know the answers and compassionate enough to understand the questions. When you find yourself discouraged, frustrated or confused, turn toward him instead of turning away, and consider what good things may come from questioning your doubts.

Acknowledgments

I want to thank Al Hsu, my editor at InterVarsity Press, for being an early champion for this book as well as a calm and wise guide throughout the entire publication process. Cindy Kiple, cover design, and Beth McGill, interior design, thank you for communicating in your design the message I endeavored to put into words. To the editorial staff, marketing team and marketing manager Deborah Gonzalez, thank you for pursuing excellence in your work.

During the research phase of this project, the librarians and staff at the Harvard Libraries, especially the Harry Elkins Widener Memorial Library, Cabot Science Library and Francis A. Countway Library of Medicine, provided superb assistance locating rare books while also making an alumna feel at home.

I am grateful to my ordination committee, who understood the value of bridge building between pastors and scientists more than a decade ago and dared to dream with me of the day when I would write a book like this one; and to my pastor, Timothy P. Schmidt, now a regional and national leader within the Assemblies of God, who never failed to believe in me.

Single-Session Discussion Guide

*(A chapter-by-chapter discussion guide is
available online at www.ivpress.com)*

The following questions are designed to help individuals and groups explore many of the intriguing themes in *Questioning Your Doubts* by Christina M. H. Powell in a single sixty- to ninety-minute session.

1. Describe a time when you needed to adjust to a new environment. Did you experience doubts about whether you belonged in this new place?

2. Have you ever felt like you inhabited two different worlds, one based on secular reasoning and the other on spiritual truths? If so, were you able to resolve this dilemma? Did you compartmentalize your beliefs and secular knowledge or attempt to integrate them?

3. In chapter two, Powell describes how compassion changes the heart of the researcher without impacting the details of experimental design. Has your faith ever changed how you view an experience while leaving the facts of the situation unchanged?

4. In chapter three, we read, "Discernment is also not an excuse to rely on feelings and hunches in place of reason and good advice." Have you ever struggled to find the right balance between feelings and reason when making a decision? What are some of the ways a person can honor both in the process of discernment?

5. If you could ask Jesus one question, what would you ask him?

6. Jesus asked many questions in his ministry. Pick one of the questions Jesus asked that are mentioned in chapter four or choose one from one of the four Gospels. What insights can you gain from this question?

7. In chapter five, Powell writes, "Many times we need to learn patience and stay seated in the stalled incline cars of life. However, some moments call for courage and initiative, and we must leave our comfort zone and climb the mountain." Name one limit you are currently facing in your life. Consider limits of resources, time and knowledge. Is the limit you are currently facing one that calls for patience or for courage? Why?

8. What truths about human life create unanswered questions? Hebrews 11:39 states, "These were all commended for their faith, yet none of them received what had been promised." What promises in the Bible were answered after the death of the person who was given the promise?

9. In chapter seven, Powell writes, "The danger to faith when things seem to go wrong in a believer's life comes from the wrong view of God. If you view God as a protective parent who will keep you from falling and scraping your spiritual knees, you will feel unloved and abandoned when life brings injury. If you view prayer as a magic formula to make your desires come true, your faith will hit a brick wall when things don't turn out according to your plans."

Can suffering enlarge our view of God? In what ways?

10. What does the gospel tell us about humankind? Why does human failure not disprove the existence of God?

11. What one change would you most like to see in your church, workplace or educational institution? What can you do to make a positive contribution toward this change?

12. In chapter nine, Powell writes, "Authentic faith relates to real life like a conversation between two friends. It is at home in the locker room as well as the cathedral." Describe two different places where you live out your faith. What does your faith look like in each setting?

13. Name an experience in your life that could serve as a "memorial stone" to remind you of God's faithfulness.

14. In chapter eleven, we read, "Both the scientific and the Christian communities include the company of scholars and the cloud of witnesses who have gone before us. Like Elisha who asked for a double portion of the blessing that had been bestowed on his mentor Elijah's life, each generation should seek to have a greater impact than the previous one." What do these two sentences tell us about the importance of mentoring? Are you presently mentoring someone or being mentored by someone? How should we view those who mentor us? What should we expect of those we mentor?

15. The author looks back on how teaching a children's Sunday school class contributed to the formation of current church leaders. Have you ever made a seemingly insignificant contribution only to find that the ripple effect enlarged your impact?

16. Spend some time this week reflecting on your current journey to this point. What are the next steps you need to take to resolve your doubts or strengthen your faith? What are you doing right now that could have a significant impact in the future?

Notes

Introduction

[1]David A. Drachman, "Do We Have Brain to Spare?" *Neurology* 64, no. 12 (2005): 2004-5.

[2]J. G. White, E. Southgate, J. N. Thomson and S. Brenner, "The Structure of the Nervous System of the Nematode *Caenorhabditis elegans*," *Philosophical Transactions of the Royal Society B: Biological Sciences* 314, no. 1165 (1986): 1-340.

[3]Pasko T. Rakic, "Introduction to the Session," *Annals of the New York Academy of Sciences* 882, no. 1 (1999): 66-67.

[4]Aaron L. Wichman, Pablo Briñol, Richard E. Petty, Derek D. Rucker, Zakary L. Tormala and Gifford Weary, "Doubting One's Doubt: A Formula for Confidence?" *Journal of Experimental Social Psychology* 46, no. 2 (2010): 350-55.

[5]Tim Woodman, Sally Akehurst, Lew Hardy and Stuart Beattie, "Self-confidence and Performance: A Little Self-doubt Helps," *Psychology of Sport and Exercise* 11, no. 6 (2010): 467-70.

Chapter 1: Created to Think

[1]Stephen Jay Gould, "Nonoverlapping Magisteria," *Natural History* 106 (March 1997): 16-22.

[2]Erwin Schrödinger, *"Nature and the Greeks"; and "Science and Humanism,"* with a foreword by Roger Penrose (New York: Cambridge University Press, 1996), p. 184.

[3]Peter Medawar, *The Limits of Science* (New York: Oxford University Press, 1988), p. 95.

[4]W. Heisenberg, "Über den anschaulichen Inhalt der quantentheoretischen Kinematik und Mechanik," *Zeitschrift für Physik* 43, nos. 3-4 (1927): 172-98.

[5]Edward N. Lorenz, "Predictability: Does the Flap of a Butterfly's Wings in Brazil Set Off a Tornado in Texas?" (paper, American Association for the Advancement of Science, Boston, 1972).

CHAPTER 2: INTERPLAY OF INFLUENCES

[1]Tom McBride and Ron Nief, "The Mindset List," *Beloit,* www.beloit.edu/mindset/.

[2]Richard Dawkins, "The More You Understand Evolution, the More You Move Towards Atheism" (paper, Edinburgh International Science Festival, 1992).

[3]C. S. Lewis, "Is Theology Poetry?" in *Essay Collection and Other Short Pieces* (HarperCollins: London, 2000), p. 21.

[4]W. H. Griffith Thomas, *The Principles of Theology: An Introduction to the Thirty-nine Articles, by the Late W. H. Griffith Thomas* (London: Longmans, Green, 1930), pp. xviii-xix.

[5]Bert Vogelstein, Surojit Sur and Carol Prives, "p53: The Most Frequently Altered Gene in Human Cancers," *Nature Education* 3, no. 9 (2010): 6.

[6]PewResearch, "Religious Landscape Survey," *Religion & Public Life Project,* http://religions.pewforum.org/reports.

CHAPTER 3: DISCERNMENT REQUIRES DOUBTS

[1]René Descartes, *The Method, Meditations and Philosophy of Descartes,* translated, with new introductory essay by John Vietch and introduction by Frank Sewall, Universal Classics Library (Washington, DC: Dunne, 1901), pp. 225, 226, 227, 233, 248.

[2]Jack Mezirow, *Learning as Transformation: Critical Perspectives on a Theory in Progress,* Jossey-Bass Higher and Adult Education Series (San Francisco: Jossey-Bass, 2000).

CHAPTER 4: SOLVING PROBLEMS WITH QUESTIONS

[1]Stephen Jay Gould, *The Richness of Life: The Essential Stephen Jay Gould,* ed. Paul McGarr and Steven Rose (New York: Norton, 2007), p. 521.

[2]Victor J. Stenger, *God and the Folly of Faith: The Incompatibility of Science and Religion* (Amherst, NY: Prometheus, 2012), p. 408.

[3]Christina M. H. Powell, "Encountering Bioethics in Everyday Ministry," *Enrichment Journal* 11, no. 3 (2006): 132-34.

[4]Andrew Pollack, "Judah Folkman, Researcher, Dies at 74," *New York Times,* January 16, 2008.

[5]"Judah Folkman: An Inspiration for the Tobin Project," *The Tobin Project,* http://tobinproject.org/about/judah-folkman.

CHAPTER 5: LOCATING LIMITS

[1]Patrick Harries and David Maxwell, *The Spiritual in the Secular: Missionaries*

and Knowledge About Africa, Studies in the History of Christian Missions (Grand Rapids: Eerdmans, 2012).

CHAPTER 8: DISILLUSIONMENT MASQUERADING AS DOUBT

[1]William Hague, *William Wilberforce: The Life of the Great Anti-Slave Trade Campaigner* (London: Harper, 2007).

[2]J. R. R. Tolkien, letter to his son, Michael Tolkien, November 1, 1963, in *The Letters of J. R. R. Tolkien,* edited by Humphrey Carpenter, assisted by Christopher Tolkien (London: HarperCollins, 1981), p. 336.

CHAPTER 10: RETRACING THE PATH

[1]Charles Robert Leslie, *Memoirs of the Life of John Constable, esq., R.A., Composed Chiefly of His Letters* (London: J. Carpenter, 1843), p. 4.

CHAPTER 11: THINKING IN COMMUNITY

[1]I. H. Hutchison, "Michael Faraday: Scientist and Nonconformist," *The Faith of Great Scientists,* MIT Independent Activities Period, January 14, 1996, http://silas.psfc.mit.edu/Faraday/.

[2]Bence Jones, *The Life and Letters of Faraday,* vol. 2 (London: Longmans, Green, 1870), p. 431.

CHAPTER 12: AN INCOMPLETE PROCESS

[1]Francis S. Collins, *The Language of God: A Scientist Presents Evidence for Belief* (New York: Simon & Schuster, 2006).

[2]Billy Graham, *A Daily Process,* Billy Graham's Devotion, October 2, 2013, http://billygraham.org/devotion/a-daily-process.

[3]Christina M. H. Powell, "Science and the Pew," *Pentecostal Evangel,* September 25, 2011, pp. 14-18; idem, "Science and the Pulpit: Ministering to Scientifically Literate People," *Enrichment Journal* 17, no. 4 (2012): 92-96.

[4]The Faraday Institute for Science and Religion, January 1, 2014, www.faraday. st-edmunds.cam.ac.uk/index.php; "DoSER (Dialogue on Science, Ethics, and Religion) Overview," *AAAS* (American Association for the Advancement of Science), www.aaas.org/page/doser-overview.